Praise for

THE GOOD DOCTOR

Case studies of grit paragons like these doctors are a great starting point
for understanding the path forward—and fun to read!

> —ANGELA L. DUCKWORTH, PHD, Christopher H. Browne
> Distinguished Professor of Psychology at the University of
> Pennsylvania and *New York Times* bestselling author of *Grit*

The Good Doctor is a great read, especially at a moment where cynicism
about our institutions and individual motivations prevail. With humanity and warmth, Tom Lee reminds us why the best physicians still view
medicine as a calling. These seven profiles are each exhilarating and
inspiring for all prospective and practicing clinicians, as well as those
seeking reassurance about the humanity of healthcare.

> —JON PERLIN, MD, PHD, President of Clinical Services
> and Chief Medical Officer at HCA Healthcare

In *The Good Doctor*, Tom Lee gets to the heart of the most pressing crisis
facing physicians today: burnout. Telling the stories of seven physicians,
he shows how each creates deeper meaning in their work and in their
lives by bringing the care of their patients to a different level, one which
resonates deeply and insulates them from our profession's stressors.
Dr. Lee's message is elegant in its simplicity.

> —LARRY H. HOLLIER JR., MD, Surgeon-in-Chief
> of Texas Children's Hospital

Dr. Lee shares the stories of extraordinary doctors and identifies the
core qualities they all display, including empathy, resilience, strong
sense of purpose, and the ability to create communities where they work.
Healthcare organizations should study these stories to understand what
motivates clinicians and what undermines those motivations, so we can
support them in doing the noble work of patient care.

> —JESSICA DUDLEY, MD, Chief Medical Officer of the
> Brigham and Women's Physicians Organization

For years we have known that burnout is largely related to dysfunctional systems and processes, not a defect in the people who dedicate their lives to heal others. Tom has beautifully tipped the scales back in the right direction via intimate storytelling about the human spirit—a spirit that rises from trauma, that heals when no cure is possible, and that loves despite all odds.

—ADRIENNE BOISSY, MD, Chief Experience Officer of Cleveland Clinic Health System

Tom Lee uses these inspirational stories to teach a powerful lesson. They show us what grit looks like and how a few individuals who find meaning in their work are having remarkable impacts.

—FREDERICK P. CERISE, MD, CEO of Parkland Health & Hospital System, Dallas

You won't be able to put this down as you get into the profiles of these seven good doctors. Tom Lee provides insights into resilience, grit, and passion, providing a framework for doctors to focus their careers to avoid burnout and to serve their patients in a meaningful manner.

—LEE SACKS, MD, retired Chief Medical Officer of Advocate Aurora Health

Good doctors like the physicians in this book inspire through their perseverance, resilience, and recognition of the need for mentoring throughout life.

—PHILIP E. STIEG, MD, PHD, Chairman and Neurosurgeon-in-Chief at Weill Cornell Brain and Spine Center

The stories of Joe Sakran and others in *The Good Doctor* show that determination and excellence have not gone out of style in medicine and are being reinvented by a new generation of physicians.

—ALLEN KACHALIA, SVP of Patient Safety and Quality and Director of the Armstrong Institute for Patient Safety and Quality of Johns Hopkins Medicine

THE GOOD DOCTOR

11/6/19

With best wishes

from

THE GOOD DOCTOR

WHAT IT MEANS, HOW TO BECOME ONE, AND HOW TO REMAIN ONE

THOMAS H. LEE, MD

New York   Chicago   San Francisco   Athens   London   Madrid
Mexico City   Milan   New Delhi   Singapore   Sydney   Toronto

1 2 3 4 5 6 7 8 9   LCR   24 23 22 21 20 19

ISBN   978-1-260-45920-3
MHID   1-260-45920-9

e-ISBN   978-1-260-45921-0
e-MHID   1-260-45921-7

Library of Congress Cataloging-in-Publication Data

Names: Lee, Thomas H.,- author.
Title: The good doctor : what it means, how to become one, and how to
    remain one / Thomas H. Lee, MD.
Description: New York : McGrawHill, [2019] | Includes bibliographical
    references and index.
Identifiers: LCCN 2019027227 (print) | LCCN 2019027228 (ebook) |
    ISBN 9781260459203 (hardcover) | ISBN 9781260459210 (ebook)
Subjects: LCSH: Physicians. | Medicine—Vocational guidance.
Classification: LCC R690 .L425 2019 (print) | LCC R690 (ebook) |
    DDC 610.69/5—dc23
LC record available at https://lccn.loc.gov/2019027227
LC ebook record available at https://lccn.loc.gov/2019027228

McGraw-Hill Education books are available at special quantity discounts
to use as premiums and sales promotions or for use in corporate training
programs. To contact a representative, please visit the Contact Us pages at
www.mhprofessional.com.

To my late father-in-law, Ali Gharib, MD,

who showed so many

what it means to be good

Contents

Acknowledgments   ix

Introduction   xi

CHAPTER
1   The Good Physician   1

CHAPTER
2   Embracing "The Hard Thing"   19

CHAPTER
3   Keeping Promises   33

CHAPTER
4   Minimizing Fear   53

CHAPTER
5   Fighting the Root Cause   69

CHAPTER
6   Treating the Whole Person   89

CHAPTER
7   Delivering Care to Those in the Greatest Need   109

CHAPTER
8 Never Giving Up 131

CHAPTER
9 Being and Becoming a Good Doctor 149

Notes 167
Index 169

Acknowledgments

THE
GOOD
DOCTOR

First and foremost, I would like to thank the seven doctors profiled in this book—Mike Englesbe, Michigan Medicine; Merit Cudkowicz, Massachusetts General Hospital; Emily Sedgwick, HCA Houston Healthcare West; Joe Sakran, Johns Hopkins Medicine; Laura Monson, Texas Children's Hospital; Lara Johnson, Parkland Health and Hospital System; and Babacar Cisse, New York–Presbyterian Hospital. They trusted me to capture their stories accurately and convey them in a way that is consistent with their values. None are self-promoters, but all could see that there were noble reasons to share the stories of their noble work.

I also want to thank my colleagues in healthcare who appreciated the idea behind this book and then pointed me toward physicians whom I *really* had to meet. For example, Laura Forese, executive vice president at New York Presbyterian, introduced me to Babacar Cisse; Fred Cerise, CEO of Parkland Health and Hospital System, introduced me to Lara Johnson; and Larry Hollier of Texas Children's Hospital introduced me to Laura Monson.

I'd like to thank friends and colleagues who have created and shared their insights about the nature of resilience and grit, two of whom deserve special mention. Deirdre Mylod, who works with me at Press Ganey, is the real thinker behind our framework for thinking about burnout, engagement, and activation. Angela Duckworth, the University of Pennsylvania psychologist (and my cousin), has created a body of work around grit that has deep and obvious influences throughout this book.

I want to thank Pat Ryan and my other colleagues at Press Ganey for encouraging and supporting the writing of this book. They are good people with good values—and they all love a good story. As each chapter was concluded, I would send the draft to about 10 of them during the next weekend, because, well, this is the kind of stuff they like to read on a Sunday morning—a way of getting ready for the week ahead.

I am grateful again to Beverly Merz for doing what she has done with all my books—serving as a trusted editor, someone who makes the manuscript better without making the author mad! I'd also like to thank Casey Ebro and her team at McGraw-Hill, for their confidence that what we thought might be a good idea actually was one, and then for their effectiveness in moving the book through the publication process so quickly.

Finally, my deepest gratitude goes to Soheyla Gharib, my wife, who has been so supportive of all aspects of my work for decades now—but who gives her greatest respect on those occasions when I prove to be a good doctor myself. She's a wonderful physician and the daughter of a wonderful physician (to whom this book is dedicated). Forty years after meeting Soheyla on the first day of our internship, I remain endlessly interested in impressing her. Nothing impresses her more than going the extra mile for a patient.

Introduction

I WISH I COULD SAY that this book began with a full-blown vision of what it means to be a good doctor in the modern era and how to become one. The reality is that it began with nothing more than the pleasure of telling a good story. And then another. And another.

The conversation that led to this book occurred in the late spring of 2018, right after Pat Ryan, the CEO of Press Ganey, learned that one of his closest friends, Sean Healey, had just been diagnosed with amyotrophic lateral sclerosis (ALS). I told Pat that I knew a wonderful ALS specialist who worked with a really excellent team—Merit Cudkowicz, MD, at Massachusetts General Hospital.

It turned out that Pat's friend had already made his way to Merit—no surprise, since in the ALS world, everyone knows who she is. She is famous among neurologists for leading clinical research trials on some of the most promising agents for this disease. She is famous among patients because she and her team offer wonderful care—and even hope—for a condition that so many others label "hopeless."

Our conversation shifted from admiration for what Merit and her team do, to amazement that they have been able to keep it up for decades for patients who are sure to have a downhill course. Merit and her colleagues remain deeply empathic with these patients and their families, even though one might expect them to have developed defense mechanisms to protect themselves from emotional involvement.

"She should be the most burned-out physician on the planet," her colleagues say. "But somehow, she is the least."

"Merit is incredible," Pat said.

"She is," I agreed. "But let me tell you about Emily Sedgwick." And then I told him how I had recently met a young breast radiologist at Baylor College of Medicine in Houston. A decade ago, when she was just in her early thirties, she re-engineered breast imaging at her institution with the goal of reducing fear. She knew that, even when women whose mammograms reveal suspicious abnormalities got their core needle biopsies the next day, it could be a very long and difficult night. So in her program 95 percent of the biopsies are done the same day. Women don't leave the mammography room right away after their initial images are taken because Emily and her colleagues know that when women get the message that more images are needed, their hearts stop. Instead, women stay in the room with the imaging equipment until a radiologist has looked at the mammograms and decided whether any other shots should be taken before the patient leaves.

"That's a great story," Pat said. I told him that there were plenty more out there. We agreed that it would be interesting to collect several of them. In an era in which so many doctors and nurses feel burned-out from their work—overwhelmed, ineffective, and depersonalized—maybe there were patterns in the stories of those who avoided burnout and lessons to be learned from them.

As soon as I began to mention that I was working on such a collection, I started getting suggestions for other remarkable physicians to interview. "You have to talk to Lara Johnson." She is the primary care physician who leads the healthcare program for homeless patients at Dallas's Parkland Health and Hospitals System. Or Joseph Sakran, who survived a serious gunshot wound to his throat when he was 17 and went on to become a trauma surgeon at Johns Hopkins. In the fall of 2018, he became nationally known after he reacted with anger to a tweet from the National Rifle Association (NRA) that physicians advocating for gun control should "stay in their lane" and started the "@ThisIsOurLane" hashtag on Twitter. But his story was already remarkable even before he tweeted, "Where are you when I'm having to tell all those families their loved one has died?" and struck a chord with so many physicians and others alarmed by gun violence.

And so on, and so on. The names poured in—and they are *still* pouring in. I did podcast interviews with the physicians profiled in this book and have continued doing so after I finished writing about the seven in this book. I'm not one bit concerned about this well running dry.

The reason to collect these stories is not to suggest to clinicians experiencing burnout that there is something wrong with them, but to offer some examples of how physicians handle the stresses that lead to burnout.

As a practicing doctor (and the spouse and father of practicing doctors), I am tuned in to the stresses and frustrations that are driving a burnout epidemic among clinicians. I hear doctors whom I really respect say that they no longer find pleasure in their work and are retiring sooner than they otherwise would have. And these are people whose sense of self is based at least in part upon the belief that they are doctors—and *good* ones at that.

But the fact is that I also meet physicians whose passion for their work endures. The physicians I profiled in this book take care of patients with the same empathy and the same high standards as the best physicians of any era. They live in the real world and are every bit as exasperated by bureaucratic hassles and information technology dysfunction as the rest of us. They don't describe themselves as "great," but they are finding greatness in their work.

These physicians are younger than I am and older than my oldest daughter (a 31-year-old cardiology fellow), and they have something to teach both of us. They are defining how to be a good doctor in our times—and showing that being a good doctor remains something pretty great. Figuring out what they have figured out and reverse-engineering their grit have yielded some insights that could help healthcare organizations shape their cultures—and might help some individuals find their way.

The individual stories were an inspiration, and the physicians behind them a delight. They are all self-aware, self-effacing, and funny. They were all amused that doing what they considered logical led them into activities that others find remarkable. The common theme to their stories is that they empathize with their patients and really want to take good care of them. And by adhering to their values, they found themselves—like Laura Monson, the craniofacial surgeon who started a summer camp for children with cleft palates—doing things that fell outside their job descriptions. None of them seem motivated by a desire for promotions, more money, or fame. What makes them remarkable are the accomplishments that have logically followed from their efforts to be a good doctor.

I realized that their collective stories were a story in themselves—with the three basic elements of that story being conflict, crisis, and resolution. For physicians and other clinicians today, the conflict is the tension between the desire to do good for their patients and the barriers, hassles, and dysfunction that slow them down and make it hard to do so. There is the gap between the life they imagined when they decided to go into medicine and the life they currently live. This conflict will be explored at greater length in Chapter 1.

The crisis is the burnout epidemic—the well-documented increase in feelings of ineffectiveness, being overwhelmed, and depersonalization that are associated with compromised quality of care and increasing rates of suicide among physicians. That, too, will be explored in greater detail in Chapter 1.

The physicians profiled in this book are not superhuman and not immune to the stresses that drive burnout. But they have found resolution by changing how they experience those stresses, which has made them more resilient. They began with the same passions that draw most people to healthcare (most notably, easing the suffering of patients), and something happened to make these passions unusually intense. As a result, these physicians have been able to persevere in their pursuit of improvement over years and decades, often doing work that falls outside of traditional patient care.

Passion and perseverance are what University of Pennsylvania psychologist Angela Duckworth describes as the key ingredients of grit. These physicians *are* gritty. They *are* great. And they *are* good. In Chapter 1, I will introduce some of the language and knowledge needed to put these physicians' stories in perspective.

And then we'll get to the good part—the stories themselves.

THE
GOOD
DOCTOR

1 | The Good Physician

WHY EXPLORE WHAT it means to be a good physician in the modern era, when there is so much to admire in traditional notions? Can we really do better than hope for empathic doctors who take pride in easing the suffering of patients and their families? Responsible people who ensure that every "i" is dotted and every "t" is crossed? Hard workers, who love what they do and will settle for nothing less than excellence in the care of their patients?

In truth, those characteristics have never gone out of style. They remain the core of the ego-identities of most physicians, nurses, and pretty much everyone else who works in healthcare. Patients hope for nothing less. But clinicians find that these noble characteristics are increasingly difficult to sustain.

The reason is a perfect storm of good news. The scientific good news is that progress has made medicine more powerful. But research advances have also made medicine more complex—in fact, so complex that no one can deliver state-of-the-science care by themselves anymore. Physicians must collaborate with colleagues even for routine conditions such as diabetes.

The demographic good news is that people are living longer, and as they do their health is dominated by chronic conditions that do not surrender easily to the right drug or the right operation, or simply working harder and longer. When numerous clinicians need to collaborate for long periods on difficult challenges, "coordination" and "compassion" become potential failings. Patients feel the effects of those failures when they occur, and caregivers are pained by them, too.

To deliver care that really meets patients' needs, good physicians need good teams around them—and that means they themselves must be good team members. That requires time, energy, emotional intelligence—and some new skills. In the old days, a good physician had to explain things well; today, a good physician has to listen well, too. Everyone on the team, physicians included, has to keep everyone else informed and pay attention to what everyone else has done.

Being a good physician today also requires use of information technology tools. There is, quite simply, too much to know. New drugs and new tests are constantly emerging, and the best ways to use them are often far from clear—even to experts. In theory, electronic medical records (EMRs) help by enabling physicians to access information about their patients and tap into the wisdom of experts. The problem is that physicians are overwhelmed by the amount of information on almost every patient and by the amount of wisdom thrust in their faces by their EMRs.

It isn't hard to understand why many physicians have focused their ire on the EMRs that bring the flood of data to them. These EMRs seem to frustrate physicians daily with small humiliations as they try to accomplish simple tasks.

I am thinking of my own recent exasperation as I tried to get rid of a reminder to give a patient a flu shot. Like many physicians, I try to do everything I am supposed to do, and a reminder to give a patient something that should benefit them bugs me until the task is completed and the reminder has disappeared. In this case, the patient had already had a flu shot at work, but to make the reminder go away, I needed to tell the EMR that the task had already been done.

I looked and looked, but I could not find a way to document that the patient had already had his flu shot. I tried clicking on this, clicking on that, and got nowhere. Finally, I saw a nurse practitioner on our team and said, with obvious exasperation, "How the hell do we document past immunizations?" She paused and then showed me a button in the middle of the task bar near the top of the screen. It said, "Document Past Immunizations."

I could swear that until that instant the button had been invisible. It was embarrassing. It was one more episode in which I was revealed to be something less than the capable, all-knowing, all-powerful healer I liked to think of myself as being.

Adjusting to using new information technology is just one of the potential insults to physicians' self-images. The widespread dissemination of medical information is another. Many people used to hold their doctors in awe and would defer to their judgments on almost anything. That's over. Today, patients do their own web searches before agreeing to go to a recommended physician or facility, or have recommended tests.

Most physicians understand that increased patient engagement with their care constitutes change for the better. Having patients learn more about their conditions and treatments, and speak up about their questions and concerns—who can be against that? But still . . . that moment of hesitation while patients weigh whether physicians' advice is worth taking can feel like part of a multipronged attack on our dignity—on our ability to feel consistently good about our work and ourselves. That makes it harder for us to sustain our passion for medicine.

The result is an epidemic of burnout and the need to understand the nature of resilience.

Burnout and Resilience

Burnout is a term tossed around loosely, and one can find wildly varying "data" on its prevalence—in part because many different definitions are in use. It isn't a disease that can be diagnosed or excluded with a lab test; it is a type of stress and is usually related to work. It is characterized by three key types of symptoms— exhaustion, feeling ineffective, and depersonalization.

Almost everyone has some of these feelings some of the time. Problems arise when their frequency increases and when symptoms of burnout spread within a society like a contagious disease. In fact, burnout is behaving like an epidemic in healthcare today— its prevalence is higher than ever in the past and still rising. And there is also evidence that the presence of burnout symptoms in one person increases the risk of development of such symptoms in others.

Burnout is more than a morale issue—it causes harm to patients as well as to the clinicians themselves. Burned-out doctors and nurses deliver care that is lower in quality and less safe. Burnout among doctors is believed to contribute to an unusually high suicide rate, but the emotional toll is real and measurable in other ways, too. For example, clinicians who are burned out are more likely to leave their jobs; why would they stay if they feel so unhappy? The financial consequences of high turnover are enormous. Some organizations estimate that every time a physician leaves, the cost of replacing that physician is one and a half times their salary due to the cost of hiring temporary help, recruiting a replacement, and the delays involved in getting the replacement credentialed with health plans, and so on. With clinical and financial stakes so high, virtually every organization in healthcare is worried about the problem of burnout in physicians.

Interest in physician burnout and concern about its impact raises the question of resilience. Why are some physicians less likely to show symptoms of burnout and more likely to remain charged up about their work through years and decades? It's as if they have been injected with a vaccine that has given them complete or partial immunity. What can the rest learn from their apparent immunity?

* * *

One thing that becomes clear as soon as one looks closely at physician burnout is that no magic bullet will cure it. More compensation isn't the answer. "Mindfulness training"—which helps clinicians "be in the moment" and thus do a better job easing the fears of their patients and receive the psychological rewards of doing so—does have some impact, but it is not enough to stem the tide alone. If there are information technology fixes that will reduce burnout, I haven't seen them yet.

The reason there is no magic bullet is that burnout is a complex multidimensional problem, with multiple causes, and thus can only be addressed through multidimensional solutions. My colleague at Press Ganey, Deirdre Mylod, developed a framework for "deconstructing" the drivers of burnout—that is, breaking them down and placing them into simpler categories that can be addressed individually. In the following figure, this framework categorizes stressors and rewards according to whether they are inherent to the role of care provider (bottom row) or are a function of external forces. Further, it acknowledges that other factors influence how individual clinicians experience the balance of stresses and rewards—that is, how resilient they might be when stresses increase.[1]

Let's start with the bottom row of the figure—the rewards and stresses inherent to taking care of patients. The fact is, it's a tough job—inherent stresses include the emotional toll of caring for suffering patients and their families, and the burden of taking responsibility for the safety and effectiveness of patients' care.

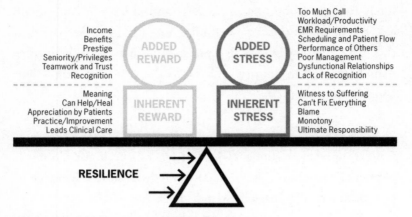

Figure 1.1   Framework for Deconstructing Burnout

This framework distinguishes rewards and stresses inherent to the role of caring for patients (bottom boxes) from those that are added (upper boxes). Resilience is a moderating influence that nudges the fulcrum to a point where more stress is bearable. EMR indicates electronic medical record.

But it's a great job, too—the inherent rewards include the respect from friends, family, and the community that results from clinicians' role in helping people, and the personal pride that comes from doing work that has meaning.

One key insight from this framework is that these inherent stresses and rewards are intertwined—that is, decreasing one's sense of responsibility or one's empathy in an effort to decrease the inherent stresses also decreases the ability to enjoy the rewards. The implication is that to improve the balance between inherent stresses and rewards, the emphasis must be on the rewards side of the figure—for example, increasing individuals' sense that their work has meaning and is respected by the people who surround them.

Keep that bottom left box in mind—we'll be coming back to it.

The upper row of the figure focuses on the external or added rewards and stresses. The term *added* is used to differentiate the inherent stresses and rewards. Most clinicians respond to descriptions of inherent stresses by agreeing, "This is what we signed up for." But when they see a list of external stresses like the burden of documentation, managing EMR systems, and coping with inefficiencies in the practice environment—they say, "No one told me I was signing up for that!" The oft-quoted estimate is that physicians spend two hours of bureaucratic catch-up work for every hour of patient care. The former represents added stress, while the latter represents what they signed up for.

External rewards are real, too, and include financial compensation, the prestige of membership in a trusted profession and affiliations with respected organizations, and positive working relationships with peers and health system leaders. However, in contrast with the inherent rewards and stresses, there is essentially no direct relationship between external rewards and stresses. For example, increased compensation cannot allay the frustration that results from a dysfunctional EMR. The implication that follows from this lack of connection between external rewards and stresses is that organizations must take on the "upper right box"—they cannot mitigate the angst that results from external stresses by increasing external rewards. Instead, organizations must show that they understand that these stresses are real and an enormous problem, and that the organization is working to ameliorate them.

Collectively, these stressors and rewards define the clinician experience, and the balance between them influences clinicians' vulnerability to burnout. But it is not the only influence. The fulcrum upon which stressors and rewards are balanced is where resilience is determined. There are some individuals for whom stressors have less impact, and there are times in any individual's life when they can better deal with stresses. In such people and in such situations, the fulcrum is moved to the right, resilience is greater and more stress can be absorbed while still experiencing the rewards of patient care and avoiding burnout.

There are thus three opportunities in this framework for reducing burnout: reducing the added stresses, enhancing inherent rewards, and increasing resilience. A key takeaway is that resilience is not the opposite of burnout; it's an improvement in the ability of clinicians to absorb the stresses that occur through their work, and not "tip over" into burnout because the stresses are overwhelming the rewards. Organizations need to reduce the added stresses and enhance inherent rewards, but they should work to improve resilience as well.

These approaches are not theoretical. An example of an organizational initiative to reduce added stress is Hawaii Pacific Health's Get Rid of Stupid Stuff (GROSS) program, through which the organization asks personnel to identify work that does not add value—such as documentation that was either never intended to be performed routinely with every encounter—or could be accomplished more efficiently in some other way. Clinicians and other personnel have been vigorously appreciative of this program. This program was described in a *New England Journal of Medicine* article in November 2018,[2] and GROSS went viral. The Cleveland Clinic had already started its GROSS program in February 2019.

Researchers at the Mayo Clinic developed and evaluated an intervention to increase inherent rewards by giving physicians a chance to talk about their work with each other. They randomized 74 physicians to two groups, both of which got an hour of protected (paid) time off every other week. The control group could use that hour however they liked. The study group spent that hour participating in small-group discussions over dinner that incorporated elements of mindfulness, reflection, and shared experience. The trial showed that physicians who participated in regular small group meetings had a 5.6 percent increase in engagement and a 15.5 percent decrease in depersonalization symptoms, while the control group had little improvement in either.[3] Based on such data, many organizations now support dinners and other gatherings that foster socialization among clinicians.

To increase resilience, interventions targeted at the individual can be helpful; for example, "mindfulness" programs have been shown to be associated with small reductions in burnout. But my belief (and it is a belief, because evidence from research in this area is sparse at best) is that a larger sustained impact can result from strengthening an individual's interpretation of their role and connection to the organization. If clinicians identify strongly with their organization and that relationship brings them pride and respect, the fulcrum moves to the right. If clinicians believe that the leaders and other personnel of the organization share values that make them proud, like a commitment to zero harm and reducing patients' fear and suffering, that also helps the fulcrum move to the right, where stress feels more manageable. But if clinicians feel like they are being used as "RVU (relative value unit) machines" by an organization that is mainly concerned with margin growth, the fulcrum moves to the left, and they are destabilized by even minor increases in stress.

Two of my favorite interventions that have strengthened a sense of "why we are here" among individuals within organizations are the Cleveland Clinic *Empathy* video and the Grady Health System turnaround campaign, "Atlanta Can't Live Without Grady."

The first was an internal training video that used scenes showing patients, family members, and caregivers on a typical day at a healthcare facility. There were no spoken words, only captions that expressed their thoughts and emotions. It ends with the question, "If you could stand in someone's shoes . . . Hear what they hear . . . See what they see . . . Feel what they feel . . . Would you treat them differently?"[4]

It was made in 2013 with $40,000 for Cleveland Clinic's personnel. At its debut showing, CEO Toby Cosgrove simply said at the end, "This is why we are here." It went viral almost immediately; nearly 5 million people have watched the YouTube version. Mention the video to anyone who has seen it, and they are likely to respond, "I still get choked up when the little girl pets the dog." Like everyone at Cleveland Clinic who watched the video, you will have established that you share the same values and that they are noble ones. You've also experienced the fulcrum moving to the right.

The Grady Health System campaign occurred during the first decade of the century when the Atlanta safety-net provider was on the verge of bankruptcy. Financial performance was only part of Grady's problems—quality and morale among the personnel were both in terrible shape. Leaders from Grady and local government developed a brilliant, moving public relations campaign with the tagline "Atlanta Can't Live Without Grady." It began with black-and-white photos of patients or prominent Atlantans (like baseball star Tom Glavine) with the Grady logo over their hearts and the "Atlanta Can't Live Without Grady" tagline. Then other images and videos of patients whose lives were saved at Grady appeared, each with the quote "I Wouldn't Be Here Without Grady." The campaign continues to this day.

Many other initiatives were undertaken to improve quality of care and business performance at Grady during this time. But talk to people who work there, and they will tell you that this campaign did more than change the way politicians and other Atlantans looked at Grady. It also changed the way Grady personnel viewed the place where they worked, and that was critical to the turnaround.

Is this real or is it hype? Here is a small "biopsy"—information posted by a former physical therapist on Glassdoor.com on June 18, 2018, about working at Grady.[5] The therapist acknowledged the stress of working there, but used the campaign slogan in the post, and ended her description of the "Pros" with "pride in the mission of serving everyone who walks through the door."

The path forward suggested by this framework is multidimensional. Organizations should work to reduce clinicians' work that isn't related to patient care, reinforce individual clinicians' ability to find meaning in their work, and define an organizational culture with values that make clinicians proud. They need to work relentlessly to reduce stress and increase rewards; they cannot just suggest to individuals that "the problem is you—you need to become more resilient." But they should understand how to measure and improve resilience, because healthcare is a field in which the unpredictable happens, well, predictably. Doctors, nurses, and other personnel need to be resilient to deal with the resulting stress.

Resilience, Activation, and Decompression

If resilience is a modulator that helps clinicians keep the rewards and stresses in balance even when there are surges in stress, what drives resilience? My colleagues at Press Ganey who were studying this issue concluded that there were two dimensions that could and should be measured—activation (the degree of an individual's engagement with their work) and decompression (the ability of an individual to disconnect from work). They developed an eight-item "resilience" tool with two separate four-item subscales and validated it by correlating its results with the Maslach Burnout Index. As you might expect, rates of burnout symptoms were lower in people whose survey responses suggested that they were more "activated" and/or better at "decompressing."

Scores are calculated for individuals based upon their level of agreement with survey questions.

The questions used to measure activation are:

1. I care for all patients equally even when it is difficult.

2. I see every patient as an individual with specific needs.

3. The work I do makes a real difference.

4. My work is meaningful.

The questions used to measure decompression are:

1. I can enjoy my personal time without focusing on work matters.

2. I rarely lose sleep over work issues.

3. I am able to free my mind from work when I am away from it.

4. I am able to disconnect from work communications during my free time.

The greater an individual's agreement with these statements, the higher his or her activation or decompression score will be. Those with higher scores have more resilience in the face of stress and are more resistant to burnout.

As more and more data become available on activation and decompression, the results have been . . . fascinating! Deirdre Mylod and I published some of them in *Harvard Business Review* in October 2018. Our article was based on data from 40 health systems on about 80,000 healthcare personnel, including about 5,000 physicians, 19,000 nurses, and 60,000 other personnel.[6] We found that all three groups had about the same average activation score (4.5), and there was a modest correlation between activation and decompression—that is, people who were better at disconnecting from their work tended to have higher activation, too. But if relaxation is good for the soul, doctors have the cards stacked against them—physicians in this analysis had lower scores for decompression compared to the other two groups.

We examined the relationships between activation/decompression and another variable—engagement—in this group. Engagement gets at issues like how satisfied individuals are as employees, whether they would recommend the organization as a good place to work or get care, and whether they are proud of the organization. Employers, including healthcare organizations, have been measuring engagement with increasing frequency in recent years, and many now report such data to their boards. Ample data demonstrate that having a workforce that is more engaged is associated with better quality, better safety, better efficiency, and better financial performance.

We found that, for both doctors and nurses, activation and decompression were important correlates of engagement—but there were subtle nuances in the types of engagement that seemed influenced by these two different components of resilience. Decompression was more strongly correlated with how nurses and physicians felt about their role as employees in an organization (based upon survey items such as "Overall, I am a satisfied employee," or "I would recommend this organization as a good place to work."). In contrast, activation was more strongly correlated than decompression with how doctors and nurses felt about their organization ("I would recommend this organization to family and friends who needed care," or "I am proud to tell people I work for this organization."). In short, decompression is related to how clinicians feel about their specific jobs, while activation is a marker for how clinicians feel about their organizations.

Recalling the framework for burnout described earlier in this chapter, think of activation as something that plays important roles in inherent rewards and the location of the fulcrum representing clinicians' resilience. Clinicians who have greater activation can reasonably be expected to have lower burnout rates and be better able to deal with surges in stress.

Initiatives to help personnel decompress are good ideas. An even better idea is to reduce preventable stress, such as Hawaii Pacific's GROSS initiative. But these ideas are neither mutually exclusive nor enough. Working to enhance the meaning that people find in their work and demonstrating that the organization's values resonate with the most noble self-images of clinicians is a critical complementary task.

Grit

The last major term to introduce as part of the modern definition of the good physician is *grit*. My tutor for thinking about grit and its implications for healthcare and physicians is Angela Duckworth, PhD, the University of Pennsylvania psychologist whose research on grit led to a McArthur Fellowship, a famous TED talk, a best-selling book, and a reunion with me. We are cousins, but she is 17 years younger than I am, and we had seen little of each other since her childhood—until 2016, when we saw each other at a meeting and started talking about grit in healthcare.

Angela's research—and her obsession—has been on people who have a goal about which they feel passionate, and then persevere in their efforts to pursue that goal over years and decades. Gritty people love what they do, and do not waver even when there are easier paths they could pursue. They are ready to sacrifice because they love what they do.

Angela has studied which cadets drop out at West Point and which hang in there. She has studied "grit paragons" in sports, the arts, and many other disciplines. And after we reconnected in 2016, we started thinking together about gritty people in medicine.

We wrote an article together in the fall of 2018 in *Harvard Business Review* entitled "Organizational Grit."[7] This article offers a framework for thinking about grit in healthcare at three different levels—the individual, the team, and the overall organization. The reason that we gave attention to teams and the overall organization was because of the changes in healthcare described at the beginning of this chapter. Medical progress has made state-of-the-science a team sport. We need teams that are more than multidisciplinary groups composed so that everyone can practice "at the top of their license." Gritty teams function like macrocosms of gritty individuals, focused on meeting their patients' needs, measuring success, and trying relentlessly to improve. And we need a gritty organizational culture, one that has clarity on the values that are most important to it and perseveres in work to pursue those values.

Thinking about gritty groups is important because an organization that hires a lot of gritty individuals is not necessarily gritty itself. In fact, because it is hard to sustain the drive to improve without encouragement from others around them, the risk of "burning out" for gritty individuals is high, unless they are immersed with other gritty individuals who are working with them, giving them positive feedback when they do good work, and negative feedback if quality slips. We describe four key elements that are important to nurture and sustain grit at all three levels (individual, team, and organization).

The first is a goal hierarchy—arrays of goals at three or more distinct levels. At the bottom are specific tasks—for example, for a primary care physician, they might include seeing patients with acute needs, tracking relevant conditions, and prescribing treatments as needed. These constitute a to-do list that, in isolation, can be a numbing inventory of tasks and a driver of burnout.

Low-level goals must track clearly and cleanly to mid-level goals (e.g., prevent complications, coordinate care, reduce symptoms) that clinicians and other personnel understand as the essential goals of their work. And above these mid-level goals there should be a top-level goal, which in isolation might seem fuzzy, abstract, and noble—like "reducing suffering." But if this top-level goal is clearly linked to mid-level goals, and those mid-level goals are clearly linked to low-level goals, then you have a goal hierarchy that can bring individuals' and organizations' passions to life and sustain them. In other words, if individuals can see how mind-numbing tasks relate to high-level goals that are important to how they see themselves, well, maybe they won't seem so mind-numbing.

Gritty people and organizations tend to have clear goal hierarchies with minimal conflict, if any, among the various goals at each level. Less gritty people and organizations have fuzziness about the overall goal, and get distracted by mid- and low-level goals that do not contribute to higher goals, or worse, conflict with other goals.

The second key ingredient is a growth mindset—the term coined by Stanford psychologist Carol Dweck for the belief that abilities can be developed through hard work and feedback. People with a fixed mindset believe that things are about as good as they can be. Gritty people with a growth mindset believe that they can get better and that they have to try to improve. Even if they might be at the top of their field, they still want to get better. They push themselves. They are chronically restless.

The third key ingredient is a resilience orientation. Gritty individuals and gritty groups pride themselves on bouncing back and learning from setbacks, and on being able to adapt to unforeseen challenges (e.g., natural disasters). Angela likes to invoke the Japanese saying, "Get knocked down seven times, get up eight." Gritty people keep getting up not because they are stupid, but because they think they can make things turn out differently this time. Thus learning and innovation are intertwined with resilience in gritty individuals.

The fourth ingredient is identification with something larger than oneself. At an individual level, that might mean identifying with a mentor. At a group level, it means individuals really think of themselves as members of the group. This means more than wearing a fleece, or a special necktie or scarf. There are values and a track record of performance that cause individuals to want to wear those fleeces, ties, and scarves.

* * *

With some familiarity with these key terms—*burnout, resilience, activation, decompression*, and *grit*—we turn now to the stories of the physicians who inspired this book. As you read them, look for how they have found meaning in their work—how a lofty, abstract notion became a clear and consuming high-level aim in their personal goal hierarchies. You will find that these physicians did not emerge from the womb gritty—they were influenced by their families and their role models. You will see a resistance to accepting the status quo and a push to improve—both personally and in the performance of their organizations. You will see a resilience—a determination to overcome setbacks.

They bring the concepts of grit to life—and, in doing so, find meaning in their work as clinicians, and help immunize others around them from the effects of burnout.

Embracing "The Hard Thing"

IN MICHIGAN AND SOME other places in the organ transplant world, there is a ritual where, before the procedure to take the organ from the deceased donor begins, everyone in the operating room pauses. Someone reads a prayer or a poem, or tells the personnel in the operating room something about the donor's life. Then for an additional 20 seconds, everyone stands in silence, not moving, not speaking. Everyone is supposed to think about the life and the loss of the person whose organ will benefit someone else, and express gratitude. After that 20 seconds, the operation can begin, and the surgeon makes the first incision to expose the organ(s) to be transplanted.

Twenty seconds of silence and immobility seems like a long time in an operating room filled with highly trained personnel revved up and itchy to move ahead. Time is their enemy, after all. They need to keep a liver or kidney or heart or lungs healthy and get them to waiting patients, who often are themselves on operating room tables in other hospitals in other cities. It shouldn't be surprising that, during these pauses, the thoughts of the surgeons and other personnel often drift to the tasks that must be done, the logistics that must go just right—or even things unrelated to the transplant that they hope to make possible later in the day.

But one weekend in 2014, Mike Englesbe found that he could not look away. During a 36-hour period, the 43-year-old surgeon at the University of Michigan went to other hospitals in Michigan three times to procure livers for transplantation. All three times, the donors were young women who had died because of opioid overdoses. And in all three cases, the path that led to the overdoses had begun with prescription pain relievers.

"When you are about to cut into the perfect bodies of three beautiful young people and remove their organs, you can't help but be affected," he says. "And a pattern like that. . . ."

That weekend changed his life. He became obsessed with understanding how prescription drugs lead to opioid addiction, and what can be done to reduce that risk. It set him on a path to becoming a leader at his institution and across his state in improving prescribing practices while continuing his role as a key surgeon in one of the busiest liver transplant programs in the country.

His story shows how empathy—even with someone who is already deceased—and a reluctance to accept things as they are can push physicians to new places that enrich their professional lives.

* * *

Mike Englesbe is a lanky former long-distance swimmer who knew he wanted to be a surgeon as a boy—and even knew he wanted to be a *transplant* surgeon. He grew up in Voorhees, New Jersey, just outside Philadelphia, the second of two children. His father worked in finance, as did his older sister eventually; his mother was a first-grade school teacher.

Sports were important in the Englesbe household. Mike's father had been a varsity basketball player at the University of Pennsylvania in an era when basketball at Penn and the other Big

Five colleges was a Philadelphia obsession. Mike's grandfather had also been a well-known athlete, and Mike's sister was quite athletic, too.

Mike grew fast and tall, and had nearly reached his adult height of 6 feet 2 inches by the age of 12. And in those early years, he had the exhilarating experience of nearly always being the best in his cohort in every sport. But by the time he was 14, others were catching up, and he realized he didn't have the talents to excel in sports like basketball that emphasized hand-eye coordination. "I wasn't good enough to be a real athlete," he recalls. "So just like everyone else on the crew team or the swim team, I flunked out of the skill sports."

Mike plunged into a sport where determination mattered most—swimming. Just as he realized he was not going to be a great basketball player, he quickly figured out that he was simply not fast enough to be a sprinter in his new sport. So he focused on long-distance events, like the mile. He moved to a private school in Philadelphia, St. Joseph's Preparatory School, and worked in long, grueling practices about eight times a week all through high school.

His sister had established a high bar. She was at the top of her high school class, excelled in sports, and went to the University of Pennsylvania. His parents supported his efforts to keep up. "Somehow, my parents let me go to swim practice a couple of days a week at 4:45 in the morning until 6:15," he says. "My dad would wait there, and then he'd drive me into Philadelphia to start school. And most days I'd come home and have another practice at the end of the day.

"In retrospect, it was really hard," he says. "I think it was probably the hardest I worked in my life. But part of the beauty of swimming is you learn you may never be the best, but if you grind it out and work hard, you can be the best you can possibly be.

"I think I'd say I was a good swimmer, and that I took my talents as far as I could take them," he says. "To have been an

Olympic swimmer, I would have had to have been three inches taller." But he was a strong enough swimmer and student to be recruited to Yale, where he swam all four years and became captain of the swim team.

Still, he says, he always knew his swimming career would end with college. He excelled at the most grueling events, like five-kilometer races in open water, but "marathon swimming" would become Olympic events only after Mike had graduated and walked away from the sport. Even though he was team captain, he knew there were better swimmers out there. But he stuck with it and never missed any of the 11 practices per week.

He went to Yale instead of other schools where he could have also been a varsity swimmer, because it was Yale. "I had to work really hard to get my A's and B's," he says. "When my dad dropped me off at college he said that I could come home if I got cancer or something—but otherwise, I had to stick it out."

* * *

Mike went from Yale to Robert Wood Johnson Medical School, the medical school for his home state of New Jersey. Despite good grades at Yale, he says, "I was pretty immature. All I did was study and swim. I never had the maturity to pause and think, 'What the hell am I doing?' But I looked at medical school differently. I realized there was much more than just taking a test and being driven.

"In my second year of medical school, it was as though a light turned on and I figured out how to be a medical student," he says. "I really got excited about the content. I'm not a man of deep curiosity, or at least I wasn't as a young person. But for the first time, I started thinking, 'This is right where I want to be.'"

The notion that he should become a transplant surgeon had first occurred to him in seventh grade, when the surgeon who had done the first heart transplant in Philadelphia came to his school. Mike started thinking it was what he wanted to do, too, but he didn't do anything specific to move in that direction until he was in medical school. "Still, I always had that as a dream, and nothing really ever changed in my mind," he says. "I always wanted to be a surgeon, and I never really pondered anything else."

Once Mike started to get a real clinical experience in medical school, he was thrilled. "I loved all my rotations in medical school," he says. "To be honest, I loved some of them more than surgery. And I can't say I loved all the surgeons I worked with. But when I was exposed to surgeons, it was clear to me that I think like these people."

He began to learn about the characteristics it would take to be a good surgeon. "You need resilience," he says. "As a surgeon, you do good things, but inevitably, really bad things happen. You can't be brought to a halt.

"The thing about surgery is that it is so humbling. You see patients, and they are so vulnerable. You try your very, very best. Sometimes, it doesn't work out, and you have to ask, 'What could I have done differently?' You have to be very self-critical, but not let it crack you. You have to see setbacks as an opportunity to do better the next time.

"I like that. I find it a virtuous existence, empowering, but very humbling—and very motivating."

The need to prioritize issues on the fly also appealed to him. "When a lot of things are going on, you have to be able to decide what to ignore," he says. "When you are doing big operations, like liver transplants, there is a lot of bleeding, a lot going on. You can't get bogged down in every detail, and you have to be able to focus on the fundamental issues. You have to be able to think about the physiology of what is happening and the technical aspects of what you can do. You have to think about what will be adequate. You don't want to do too much, and you don't want to do too little."

He was pretty sure he could persevere through the nine years of hard work and low pay that would constitute his surgical training. "I figured if I can swim six hours a day year after year, I can do surgical training," he recalls. "That kind of work appealed to me. Liver transplants can be a 12-hour slog, and I kind of like to do the really hard thing."

* * *

Mike went to the University of Michigan Health System for his internship and residency. A fellowship in multiorgan transplantation followed. During a rotation at the VA Ann Arbor Healthcare System, he met a medical resident, Audrey Wu, and they married two years later. Today, Audrey also works at the University of Michigan, focusing on patients with heart failure, many who need cardiac transplantation. They have three children—two daughters and a son.

When they met, Audrey was headed to the University of Washington for cardiology training, so Mike interrupted his clinical fellowship at Michigan and arranged a two-year research fellowship there, too. (Top surgical training programs frequently include two-year research blocks.) "I studied aortas in baboons for two years," he says. "It was vascular biology research. It was a great experience, and I met nice people and learned a lot. But it wasn't my kind of thing."

He knew what his kind of thing was. He liked transplants. Kidneys were good; livers even better. And that is what he focused on when he returned to Ann Arbor.

* * *

In the years after his return to Michigan, something else emerged as Mike's "kind of thing"—teaching. His mother was a teacher, and one of his grandfathers was a professor, so he saw teaching students and residents as a reflection of his family's values. Even though he was technically still a trainee, he joined the Education Advisory Committee for the Department of Surgery upon his return. In the ensuing years, he assumed increasing educational responsibilities—he estimates he spends a third of his time on education. He won a succession of awards for his teaching and played a leadership role in the recent implementation of a new curriculum at the medical school.

"I'm a good surgeon, but it's not like I'm Toby Cosgrove," he says, alluding to the recently retired CEO of the Cleveland Clinic, someone who was widely considered the top cardiac surgeon in the country during the period when Mike was training. "And I'm a good scientist, but I know I'm not going to win a Nobel Prize. As for the education piece—I'm not sure exactly why, but it's been natural for me. I've always really, really liked the students and trainees, and enjoyed their success."

He also started to win awards for the softer side of patient care. He was the University of Michigan Nominee in 2012 for the Arnold P. Gold Foundation Humanism in Medicine Award and won the Leonard Tow Humanism in Medicine Award at his medical school that same year. "I think I got more credit than I deserved," he says. "I am a kind of tall person and a transplant surgeon, and people aren't necessarily expecting normal human interactions from someone who fits that stereotype.

"Around that time, my social network of people at my institution from students up through faculty had really grown," he says, recalling the pleasure added by this new dimension of his professional life. "I really knew what was going on in a lot of their lives. We have 170 medical students per class, and I wrote 40 residency letters of recommendations one year. I've gotten busier and been given other things to do, but I really enjoyed that period when I could go deep with so many young people. I grew a lot in those years when I was starting to do this work, and I still really enjoy it."

* * *

Without any particular plan, these various strands of Mike's professional life—his skills as a surgeon, his interest in young people, his readiness to admit when something was just not right—came together that Sunday in 2014 when he was on call for the liver transplant team. His role that weekend was to go out and bring the donor livers home, while one of his colleagues was preparing the recipient to receive the new organ. The three procurements took about a day and a half.

The first donor was a young woman who had overdosed on opioids. The story that came out during the pause to honor her was that she had had a sports injury and basically never been the same afterward. She got hooked on opioids and eventually overdosed. The second was another young woman with essentially the same story, but beginning with a wisdom tooth extraction. And the third was a young woman who had just graduated from high school and gone to a graduation party to which someone brought prescription opioids. She experimented, overdosed, and died.

Michigan had only recently made the pause to reflect on the donor's story a standard part of the transplantation procedure, and the impact on Mike was profound. "Any physician is going to be affected by seeing young people who are very sick, dying, or have died," he says. "But this situation couldn't be more powerful. There's a naked donor on the table, and you're hearing the story of this young person's journey to death.

"Among transplant professionals, there really is deep and sincere gratitude for the gift of an organ," Mike says. "Everyone takes it very seriously. Hearing these three stories in a row was shocking. I couldn't stop thinking about them."

* * *

Mike could see that although the availability of these three livers was good for the recipients of these organs, it was also the sign of a devastating public health problem. "I became very interested in seeing if there was anything I could do to try to combat this, at least in my region," he said. "But I didn't know where to start."

He talked to two of his closest friends—Chad Brummett, an anesthesiologist who focused on pain management, and Jennifer Waljee, a plastic surgeon and health services researcher. Both had been working on the opioid epidemic. He asked if he could join them in this work.

They first turned to the challenge of caring for patients coming in for surgical care who were already chronic users of opioids. "These people are very hard to care for," Mike said in a 2018 talk at a NEJM Catalyst meeting. "Opioid use and misuse, addiction, pain—these are complex problems. I immediately became humbled by the appreciation of the remarkable, almost mythical grip that opioids can have on people."

Brummett suggested that they needed to pivot in their work and focus on keeping healthy people healthy—to prevent new persistent chronic opioid use. "We learned that most heroin users, most people who overdose, get their introduction to opioids from someone like me, or from a dentist after a wisdom tooth extraction, or from an orthopedic surgeon after a sports injury," Mike said. "So we dug in.

"When you and your friends have a good idea and are motivated, it's amazing what can happen," Mike says. They discussed their goals with colleagues at the University of Michigan's Institute for Healthcare Policy and Innovation (IHPI), as well as with other researchers, policy experts, public health officials, and leaders of Blue Cross Blue Shield of Michigan and Michigan Medicaid. "Everyone was helpful. Everyone wanted to collaborate. And we began to understand this problem."

They were stunned to learn that 6 percent of patients who have surgical care become new chronic opioid users. "Becoming a new chronic opioid user is probably the most common surgical complication in the United States," Mike began saying in his talks.

The numbers are even higher for some subsets of patients. For example, 20 percent of women with breast cancer who receive systemic therapy, radiation, mastectomy, and reconstruction finish that journey as chronic opioid users. Jennifer Waljee wrote a paper showing that 5 percent of adolescents who have surgical care become chronic opioid users.

"Needing opioids every day can happen to any of us," Mike realized. "The usual story is, 'I had my wisdom teeth removed or I had surgery on my knee. I took the opioids for a couple days, then I stopped. Then I felt really bad, so I took some more, and that continued.' Since people in the United States have an average of nine procedures over the course of their lives, we are all at risk for this complication."

* * *

Describing the root cause of the opioid epidemic was not enough; Mike and his colleagues wanted to figure out how to fix the problem. "And that is where our partnerships became key," Mike says.

Here, Mike's deep relationships with students and trainees came in handy. A medical student and a resident did a study in which they interviewed every patient at Michigan Medicine who had undergone a laparoscopic cholecystectomy (gallbladder removal). They noted how many pain pills they were given at discharge, and how many patients actually took. The average number of pills received was 45; the average number taken was 6. That meant 39 pills, on average, were available to cause overdoses like those that killed Mike's three donors that weekend.

The student then made a five-minute video for all Michigan Medicine surgeons and residents. It presented the data and posed the question, Why not prescribe just 15 pills? And since then, every patient having a laparoscopic cholecystectomy has received 15 or fewer pills. "And something interesting has happened," Mike says. "Patients are taking only about two pills. And they report their pain care as good if not even better." Based on these findings, they have developed new pill protocols, and many patients recover from procedures without needing opioids at all.

"This little experiment became the basis for our strategy to transform postsurgical opioid prescribing in our state, and hopefully, the United States," he says. "In Michigan, we're very lucky that we have this amazing platform funded by Blue Cross Blue Shield, which allows physicians to lead quality improvement across the surgical world in the entire state. We can now ask patients across the state: How many pills did you get? How many did you take? How was your care? Did you get adequate pain care?

"It turns out, if you get a huge bottle of pills, you take a lot of pills," he says. "If you get a few, you just take a few. Your pain care essentially is the same.

"Right-sizing opioid prescribing is relatively low-hanging fruit," Mike says. "But the story is not as simple as just writing prescriptions for fewer opioids." The goal is to learn how to do procedures with no opioids at all in patients who can get by without them.

* * *

Mike continues to think of his primary work as being a liver transplant surgeon. When at work, he is still most at home with his hands deep inside someone's abdomen.

But the same drive to improve that allowed him to get everything he could from his talents as a swimmer has pushed him to do all he can for patients—even the ones who have died and given their organs to others. And the pleasure he gets from teaching has turned him into a key leader in quality improvement, especially regarding opioid prescribing, in his institution and beyond.

Mike became codirector of the Michigan Opioid Prescribing and Engagement Network in 2016 and the director of the Michigan Surgical Quality Collaborative in 2017. He and his colleagues have a goal of performing 50 percent of Michigan's outpatient procedures without opioids while improving pain care at the same time.

Mike and his colleagues identified just how many pain pills patients should receive after 15 common procedures. The recommendations were introduced in October 2017; in the next six months, opioid prescribing after surgical care in Michigan dropped by 20 percent.

"Certainly, Michigan's a safer place today than just a few years ago," he says. "I hope I never again have to do three donor operations in a row in the same day. But if I do, I am confident that, in Michigan, the donors won't be three beautiful young people who overdosed on opioids."

He is proud of this work, but shrugs off accolades and emphasizes his good fortune to be in the right place at the right time. "I work at the University of Michigan," he says. "We feel a deep commitment to serving the 10 million people in the state of Michigan. We're a good hospital. We have a lot of resources. We understand care pretty well. When we have something that we think could benefit the rest of the state, we have a lot of resources from Blue Cross Blue Shield and our own institution to try to drive improvement."

Asked why he, who spent nine years becoming a transplant surgeon, is giving so much time to what is essentially a public health problem, he pauses. "It's a great question," he says. "I think all of us—we seek impact. We seek meaning. We seek purpose. For me, I get a lot of my energy from two things. One is the people I work with, like my friends Chad and Jen, and all these students and residents, and the patients, of course. Two, I feel a strong obligation with all the opportunities that I have had to serve the people of Michigan.

"Sure, it takes a toll on some other aspects of your life," he concedes. "But you try to balance those things out. Taking care of one patient at a time is not enough. You have to be thinking about how your patient got to where they are, and what you can try to prevent that from happening to someone else and improve on the care for the next patient.

"I feel like I have had every opportunity," he says. "If I can't be successful in making the world a better place, who can?"

3 | Keeping Promises

THE TERM *patient centered care* can seem rhetorical without examples that bring it to life. That is why I usually begin my talks on this topic by showing an email from Merit Cudkowicz, MD, from Saturday afternoon, January 16, 2016.

Merit is the chief of neurology at Massachusetts General Hospital (MGH) and a leading expert on one of neurology's most feared degenerative diseases—amyotrophic lateral sclerosis (ALS). That morning, I had written Merit on behalf of a friend of a friend—someone with newly diagnosed ALS. The patient had learned on the Internet about a promising new stem cell treatment that had been developed in Israel and was being tested in a few sites around the world, one of which was MGH.

He was desperate to see if he could get into the trial, trying everything he could think of. He contacted a mutual friend, Sven, who worked in healthcare, and asked if he knew someone, anyone, who could help. Sven contacted me, and I contacted Merit. Three hours later, Merit wrote back to Sven and me:

Dear Sven and Tom,

We recently completed enrollment in the US phase 2 trial of NurOwn (Brainstorm)—the same treatment reported by Hadassah. The study in Hadassah was the first study— phase 1—it was small, dose finding, uncontrolled. While I really hope they are right in their interpretation of the results, I think it isn't yet so clear. The US study enrolled 48 participants, using the highest concentration of cells used in the Hadassah phase 1 trials. We should have results late spring, I hope.

There are a lot of other options now—the science in ALS has really taken off—thank goodness! And there are a lot of great ideas and targets. We would be available to talk to your friend—either in person or by phone—to go through some of these. If your friend agrees, please connect him directly with me and Katie (cc'd above), who is our research access nurse.

We are here to help your friend.

Merit

The title that I use on the slide showing this email is "What We Are After in Seven Words," alluding to the last seven words of Merit's message: "We are here to help your friend." I say to clinicians in the audience that I know all of them are under duress, and many of them are skeptical that "patient experience" is important. But then I ask if anyone in the room doesn't consider Merit's closing phrase as core to their notions of excellence?

No one pushes back. Her email provides a reminder that, even when the chances are small that medicine can extend life or improve health, even when everything that can be done has been done, physicians still have important roles to play. In fact, *everyone* in healthcare whom I have met wants to convey Merit's message,

"We are here to help your friend." And most agree that this message is most important when there is little that can be done to change a patient's course.

ALS is the most common neurodegenerative disease affecting the motor neuron system. The onset typically occurs when people are in their forties and fifties and start to show signs of a gradual degeneration of motor neurons in the brain and spinal cord. They usually become totally paralyzed, and most die from respiratory complications within two to five years of diagnosis. There is no known cure for ALS, although a few medications slow progression in some patients and have been approved for use in this condition.

Three years after this email, research on ALS therapies is showing promise, and there is a real sense that the outlook in ALS may be about to change. The great excitement these days is about newer agents like NurOwn, which attack ALS in fundamentally new ways. This isn't the first time in the past two decades that Merit and other ALS clinicians have been excited by research advances, but they were usually to be disappointed by further studies. You can see in her email her efforts to temper enthusiasm and keep hopes realistic. ("While I really hope they are right in their interpretation of the results, I think it isn't yet so clear.") But talk to Merit these days about what is happening in ALS, and you come away thinking, "This time, it might be different."

What drew her to caring for patients with a condition for which other physicians have often said, "There is no hope"? When she hears that from patients, why does she immediately say, "That simply isn't true"? How has she sustained her ability to convey messages like "We are here to help your friend"?

"She should be the most burned out physician on the planet," one of her colleagues says. "But somehow, she is the least."

* * *

Merit Cudkowicz's parents and her older sister arrived in the United States in 1959, via a boat from Italy. Her father was a researcher in immunology, and the family had moved to Oak Ridge, Tennessee, where he would do postdoctoral research, and where they would have their other two children. First, there was a boy, and then Merit was born in 1963. (Merit's last name is pronounced suh-KOH-vitch; her grandfather on her father's side emigrated from Poland to Italy in the early 1900s.)

Merit's parents planned to be in the United States only a year or two. They had both grown up in Milan, loved Italy, and fully expected to return. Merit's mother didn't speak English when they arrived in the United States. "It was quite a culture shock for them," Merit says. "My mom likes to tell a story about how they tried to kick her out of a restaurant once. She was dressed in what was a fancy Italian style, and they thought she might be a prostitute or something."

By the time Merit was two, her parents had decided to stay in the United States, and Merit's father found an academic position at the University of Buffalo, pursuing immunology research on natural killer cells and bone marrow transplants. Buffalo is where Merit and her siblings spent most of their childhoods.

When she graduated from Amherst Central High School in 1981, her yearbook entry said that she wanted to be a neurologist. She has no memory of why she thought or wrote that, but she was definitely interested in science and recalls a heavy emphasis on academics in her household. "My parents did not let us go into sports, and strongly discouraged us from even being athletic," she recalls. "I only joined my first sports team in the spring of 2018. I'm part of a soccer league here in Boston and got my first jersey ever. My mom lived nearby, and I went over to show it to her."

Merit was accepted via early decision to MIT and headed to Cambridge, Massachusetts, intending to become a nuclear engineer. It was 1981, a period when worldwide oil shortages were causing long lines at gas stations. "Everybody was thinking about how to make new energy," she says. "I was excited about that."

But when she took the entry class for nuclear engineering, she was the only woman in the room. The subject matter also did not click for her. "It didn't grab me," she says. "I moved toward chemical engineering, and I loved it. The material I liked was what is known as biomedical engineering today, and I met a lot of people who were interested in biology and medicine. It was a common major for students who would go on to medical school. But I wasn't thinking medicine. I was thinking research. I always thought that, like my father, I would be in the lab full time."

Merit soon felt she had come to the right place and not just because of classroom experiences. "I loved MIT," Merit says. "It was hard—much harder than medical school. But it was fun, and people were really into what they were doing."

She remembers how, early on, all the freshmen lined up to meet the president of MIT. To pass the time as they waited, many of the students were playing with Rubik's cubes, the three-dimensional puzzles. Merit had never seen one before, but immediately rose to the challenge. "You had to solve the Rubik's cube to have street cred," she says. She wasn't one of those geniuses who solved it in 30 seconds; it took her a couple of months, but she got it done. (NB: It took Ernō Rubik, the inventor of the puzzle, over a month the first time he solved it.)

* * *

As exhilarating as that first year at MIT was, it turned tragic toward the end with the death of her father. He had developed stomach cancer. Merit learned of his diagnosis very late in his course and in an unusual way—from her French teacher at MIT.

"There is this very Italian thing—trying to hide what's going on from your kids. He didn't want our studies to be interrupted," she says. Her parents had called the school to ask them to keep an eye on her during the difficult times that lay ahead, and one of her teachers decided to let her know that something was going on. Decades later, that experience would be one reason she and her colleagues at MGH started a "parenting program" for ALS patients, in which a noted child psychiatrist, Paula Rauch, helps parents talk to their children about ALS.

* * *

There was no single moment that led Merit to decide that she would go to medical school rather than pursue a PhD in laboratory science. As an undergraduate, her goal was research, and she was driven by a vague, idealistic notion that she would be happy as long as she was able to contribute knowledge that would do good. She was no longer trying to be a nuclear engineer and solve the energy crisis, but was increasingly oriented toward biological science.

Sometime during her sophomore and junior years at MIT, she began to get advice that going to medical school and getting an MD would provide more flexibility than going for a PhD, and that she would have more opportunities and options for how she pursued research. Her advisor at MIT was Robert Langer. As she puts it, "That was before he was super famous, back when he was just a little famous." Langer was well on the way to becoming arguably *the* most influential biotechnology researcher in the world, making major advances in drug delivery systems and tissue engineering. Excited by the work of Langer and other biomedical engineers, Merit applied for a program that would allow her to go to Harvard Medical School and continue studies and research at MIT (the Harvard–MIT Program in Health Sciences and Technology, or HST).

She got off to an inauspicious start—failing her very first examination at medical school, an anatomy test. "It was probably the best possible time to fail—at the beginning," she says. "At

MIT, every test was open book. I never had to memorize a thing. It was really about problem solving and thinking. I had to adjust to the fact that in medicine there *is* a lot of information that you *do* have to absorb and retain."

Merit lagged behind in adjusting to the medical school culture in other ways. "In retrospect, one problem was that I didn't live on campus," she says. "I loved being at MIT so much that I continued living in Cambridge, instead of with the other medical students on the Boston side of the river. I didn't realize how competitive medical school was. Even during hurricanes and storms, people would go into the anatomy lab and study. The result was that I just wasn't prepared."

One of the key ingredients of grit, as I mentioned earlier, is a resilience mindset; gritty people learn from setbacks, and that is what Merit did. She sat down with the professor who led the anatomy course, discussed what had happened and how she could do better, and she quickly turned her performance around.

A year later, she was in love—with neuroscience. "It was taught by Mike Moskowitz," she recalls, referring to the MGH neurologist/stroke researcher. "It was really, really fun. And there was this excitement building about the brain, and where it was going, and the potential for big things happening."

That sense that big things were about to happen in neurology was something new. During the previous few decades, research had led to advances in treatment of cardiovascular disease (coronary artery bypass graft surgery, coronary angioplasty, and cholesterol lowering drugs) and cancer (chemotherapy, bone marrow transplants). In these areas, incurable diseases had become treatable, and sometimes curable.

In neurosciences, too, research was advancing knowledge, but those advances had not yet led to treatments that could significantly extend life or improve health for patients with strokes, brain tumors, or degenerative conditions like ALS. One joke often told by non-neurologists was "What is the title of the shortest book in the world?" The answer was *Neurological Therapeutics*. The implication was that there was little one could actually do to treat neurological conditions.

Neurologists were not amused by that joke, of course, and told the physicians making that joke that they were dead wrong (at least, that is what they said to me when I would make that joke). Researchers were getting a deeper and deeper understanding of the physiology (how things worked) and pathophysiology (what was happening when things broke down) of the nervous system. And the ability to study DNA was opening an exciting new door, allowing researchers to define the genetic bases of degenerative diseases like Alzheimer's disease, Huntington's disease, and ALS.

Progress against these conditions made neuroscience seem like a wide-open field. Merit thought, "I want to be part of this."

* * *

What she had not anticipated was that she was going to love patient care. When she got to her third year of medical school, she started her rotations through the various disciplines of medicine. Many researchers viewed clinical training as a distraction from the work that really mattered, which was laboratory research. "But I really liked seeing patients," she says. "I liked sharing their stories and doing things that helped them."

As much as she enjoyed her first real experiences in patient care, she did have some problems adjusting to hospital life. Merit was *still* living in Cambridge, in a rent-controlled apartment halfway between MIT and Harvard Square, and most of her rotations were across the Charles River, at MGH. "On my surgery rotation, I had to be at the hospital to start rounding on patients at 5 a.m.," she recalls. "I missed a few rounds because it was so early, so I used to have my mom wake me up. She was very loyal, and she would call me on the telephone to make sure I was up in time."

Merit did neurology as a "core clerkship" during her third year at MGH, and then as an advanced elective during her fourth year at Brigham and Women's Hospital. "It felt like I was going back to problem-solving," she says. "It was about trying to figure out where the lesion is and what's going on with the patient. The teachers were these giants of neurology, like C. Miller Fisher and Raymond Adams. They spent a lot of time thinking about each individual patient, and I liked that part."

Merit decided that neurology was for her, but she was still thinking that she would become a laboratory-based scientist—mainly because that was what she had been immersed in throughout her education. At that point, she didn't know anything about *clinical* research—conducting trials with patients to determine what treatments might help them. She took an extra year during medical school, going into the laboratory to study Huntington's disease—a rare but terrible inherited disorder that results in progressive degeneration of brain cells and is perhaps best known for claiming the life of folk singer Woody Guthrie. She spent that year slicing brains, looking for different protein aggregations that might help unravel the basic biology of the disease.

* * *

Merit arrived in neurology at an exciting moment. In the early 1990s it seemed like every year there was a discovery of a genetic mutation behind a major neurological disease, like Alzheimer's or Huntington's. The same was occurring in other fields, for diseases like cystic fibrosis and many cancers.

"There was this buzz in neurology that therapeutics were just around the corner," she says. "That is what got me excited about neuro-degeneration—the chance that we might finally be able to do something for these terrible conditions. Naïve or not, we thought there was finally something to hang our hats on.

"I really wanted to be a neuro-degeneration person rather than someone focusing specifically on ALS," she says. "I was excited about all those areas—a lot of the genes had been discovered by researchers at MGH, so we were talking about these diseases all the time. MGH had just started a fellowship focusing on neuro-degenerative disorders, and I started seeing patients with all those conditions."

Merit found that, as a doctor, she had the right personality for taking care of patients who—all too often—had a steady downward course. "I always liked chronic conditions," she says. "I did not want to run a code. I was more into seeing people as outpatients, thinking about them, and making long-term plans.

"And I fell in love with ALS patients," she says. "That is what caused me to steer more in that direction rather than toward the other diseases."

* * *

It was one patient in particular who caused Merit to make ALS the dominant focus of her work—and they met because of research underway at MGH. A major genetic breakthrough occurred in 1993, while Merit was working as chief resident in neurology at MGH. An MGH neurologist, Robert ("Bob") Brown, led an international team that discovered the first ALS-associated gene. They found that a mutation in a gene called SOD1 was present in 10 to 20 percent of patients with the inherited forms of ALS (which account for about 10 percent of ALS cases), and MGH soon began trying SOD1 infusions into the cerebral spinal fluid bathing the brain and spinal cord in the hope that it might arrest the disease.

In 1995, Merit became involved—deeply involved—in the care of a family in which three of five adult siblings had developed ALS symptoms around the same time. They had inherited the SOD1 mutation from their mother, who had already died from

ALS. They had come to MGH because they wanted to participate in research trials. They knew that experimental treatments like SOD1 infusions might not help them (and, as it turned out, they did not have any impact). But they understood that research was essential if anything was to help the next generation of ALS patients, which could very well include their own children.

Merit started spending a lot of time with the three, all of whom were elementary and middle school teachers who lived in Connecticut. She really liked them and admired their courage, dignity, and generosity. As they got sicker, it was harder and harder for them to come to Boston, and Merit didn't want to just take phone reports on how they were doing. "I wanted to see them," she says. "So I started driving there to give them care in their homes. That was how I started to learn about what life was *really* like with ALS."

The particular genetic mutation that these siblings had inherited had a 100 percent penetration rate—that is, every person who inherits the mutation gets the disease. And with this mutation, the downhill course is rapid—it's terminal in about nine months unless the patient is placed on a ventilator. One of the three, Susan, chose to go on a ventilator; she had a young son who was just eight years old and wanted to be there for him as long as possible.

Susan was in her early forties, about a decade older than Merit at that point, and she had a powerful effect on the young neurologist. Merit was just about to get married to a mathematician named Eugene Sorets, whom she had met seven years before in Buffalo. Their family life was about to begin. They would have a son in 1996 and a daughter in 1998.

"Susan *really* wanted to live for her son and her husband, who was a fabulous man who was in the military. They were very much in love," Merit recalls. "She just felt that Bob Brown and I could solve this ALS thing eventually. She said she wanted to be able to go in peace knowing that, by the time her son was of the age that he might be at risk, we would have a treatment for it. It wasn't just for her son, but also her nieces, nephews, and all the people with ALS.

"So she asked me something point blank. She asked me to promise her that I wouldn't abandon ALS," Merit says. "She said I had to promise to stay in it. By then, I was fully hooked, so I said yes, of course."

* * *

Merit kept her promise. Bob Brown was leading the ALS center at MGH, which included a couple of other physicians besides Merit and a nurse. Merit became the co-director of the ALS Center in 1998, and the director in 2008 when Brown left MGH for the University of Massachusetts. In 2018, the center was renamed the Sean M. Healey & AMG Center for ALS at Mass General after a major donation from and in honor of the business leader who had recently been diagnosed with ALS and had become Merit's patient.

By this point, the center had grown to include more than 100 faculty and staff, including eight neurologists, several nurse practitioners, physical therapists, speech therapists, a chaplain, and a social worker, as well as researchers. It had become the world's largest hospital-based research program for the disease; patients knew that they would get compassionate and excellent care, and the chance to participate in research trials with the latest treatments.

Insurance reimburses only a fraction of the care patients receive at the center; the rest is covered by MGH and philanthropy. The donation made in Healey's honor is expected to be a game-changer, allowing expansion of research and improvement of the care received by ALS patients.

The care at the center shows what is possible when clinicians focus on their patients' needs, even when those patients have little chance of recovering their health.

"The clinic model has changed a lot and, actually, I'm super proud of it," Merit says. "We hear from our patients what their needs are. We started a house-call program—first just adding home visits on the edges of our day, but then realizing that we needed a fully staffed program. Today, we take care of about 100 patients at home. We try to do that in between their visits to the office, so that instead of being seen every three months, they are seen every six weeks. We started this based on feedback from patients. They said that they felt like they would come to clinic, we would tell them all this stuff, and then we wouldn't see them for three months, during which lots was happening that we might have been able to do something about."

The center provides care for about 500 patients with ALS. Routine visits last two to three hours, during which patients have access to neurologists, a palliative care physician, a pulmonary specialist, nurses, and a respiratory therapist, speech therapist, physical therapist, and social worker. "The social worker was added because patients said they were just inundated by insurance and other issues that they needed help with," Merit says. "It's not a counseling social worker; it's more of a resource role.

"It's a real team approach," she says. "Patients don't see everyone on every visit, but they see who they need to see based on their symptoms. They know that they can reach any of them at any time. And there is always somebody on hand 24/7 to answer the phone when they call."

Merit and her colleagues are doing more and more virtual medicine. "I'm a huge fan of tele-visits," she says. "I don't have to examine the patient that much after they are diagnosed. If I have to examine them, we can get them in. But by the time they get dressed, come to MGH, and park, they are exhausted. The tele-visits are a way to see them in their home and cover most of the same things that we would talk about in person.

"We like to give patients a choice," she says. "We ask them whether they want to do a tele-visit, or a house visit, or come in person. People do a mixture, depending on where they live and where they are in their illness."

One of the newer members of the team is a psychiatrist, Paula Rauch, who focuses upon helping patients talk to their children about their condition. "Most of our patients are in their forties or fifties, and they have young kids," Merit says. Recalling how late in her father's illness she learned how sick he was, she is attuned to the difficulty of these family issues, and frequently says, "We take care of 500 families"—as opposed to 500 patients.

"The patients and their spouses often ask us, 'When do we tell our kids? How do we tell our kids?' None of us have any training in that," Merit says. "Paula is a psychiatrist who has been actively doing this with cancer patients. She's not coming here to be the psychiatrist for our patients. It's really about helping them know what their kids are ready for and how to listen to their kids, and how to respond when the kids offer some opening. It's very individualized. I don't know that we can learn to do what she does, but at least it gives us some tools to help."

* * *

Clinic day, when most of the return visits are scheduled, is Tuesday. New patients come on Monday or Friday, because Merit and her colleagues realize that it is devastating for someone with newly diagnosed ALS to see a waiting room filled with patients with ALS across the range of disability caused by the disease. Regardless of how thoughtful the scheduling is, the experience is hard on patients, and it's hard on staff, too.

Merit gets angry when she hears that patients have been told there is nothing that can be done. "That's devastating, and it sucks the air out of them—and it's just not true," she says. "There are actually four drugs approved somewhere in the world for people with ALS, and there are maybe 20 trials, and there's a big pipeline. I tell them that there are actually thousands of people working on ALS right now, and that our job not only is to take really good care of them day-to-day, but make sure that they know about trials so they can make their choices.

"That's the other thing about our center. We want people to know that they have options. We never do a trial that we don't think has a good scientific rationale. They're all good options, decent options.

"Even if our trials don't work, we're still doing things for people with the care we give," she continues. "I've had lots of trials that have not worked, and it's devastating for everybody involved. But it's always the patients who keep our spirits up. I have a couple of quotes I keep from my patients, 'Thanks for trying. Don't give up. What's the next trial I can be part of?'

"If they can keep up, we can keep up somehow."

* * *

Despite the hope that research creates, burnout *is* an issue at the center. "It's a bigger problem for our nurses, because they have a different relationship with the patients," Merit says. "We often see patients back-to-back—first the doctor, like me, and then one of our nurses—and we hear completely different stories. When I am seeing the patient, they want to hear all about the research, what trial they can be on. The focus is on the hope. When they see the nurse, they'll tell them all the stuff that's going on in the house and all their fears. By the end of the clinic, the nurses are actually pretty wiped out and devastated.

"It's not that we physicians don't care," Merit continues. "It's just that we're not hearing the same level of emotion. When someone tells me something really intimate, I feel privileged to have won that patient's confidence. The best compliment I ever got from a patient was that I had a heart of a nurse. She was a nurse herself.

"I think if I was not engaging them in research but only seeing patients and focusing solely on the reality of what was happening to them and their families, I could see getting burned out."

That's why every Tuesday after clinic, members of the ALS team walk out of MGH and meet in a nearby restaurant for a bite or a drink and conversation before going home. "Maybe five or six of us go out each time," Merit says. "The group varies, but everyone knows they can come if they want. The idea is just to unwind. Sometimes we see 40 or 50 people in a day. They see different doctors, but the rest of the team is seeing everybody who needs them. The nurses and speech therapists might see 20 or 30 people.

"It can be emotionally hard. It *is* emotionally hard. We don't talk about the patients. We just unwind."

* * *

There was a time when Merit herself felt a bit burned out. Back around 2012, she had three studies going and was convinced that all three would work. There were two large late-stage trials for treatments of sporadic (noninherited) ALS, and a promising new approach to the SOD1 mutation—the one that had caused the death of Susan, her siblings, and her mother. The first two trials were negative, and the third treatment was stopped when it was found to cause toxicity in animals.

"I actually started to lose a little hope here," she recalls. It was around that time that she was invited to become chair of the department of neurology at MGH—a huge honor, but one that came with a lot of management responsibility.

"So I did step back a little from ALS—not from taking care of patients, but a little from day-to-day research," she says. "I spent more time mentoring others to lead the trials. I also wanted to get some perspective and think about what we needed to do to have research trials that were less likely to fail. In other words, fewer trials but with better chances."

* * *

Today, Merit and her husband live in the same house that they bought when Merit was a neurology fellow back in the 1990s and where they raised their two children. Her husband, Eugene ("He's awesome."), works in finance. Her son is a senior at Cornell, majoring in biomedical engineering and having the opposite of his mother's initial college experience—he is one of the only men (30 of 35 students are women). He intends to go to graduate school and is interested in drug development and delivery—the kind of work that made Merit's undergraduate advisor, Robert Langer, famous. Their daughter is at Brown, studying neuroscience and planning on going to medical school.

And Merit didn't stay out of the mix for long. ("Now, I'm back!" she says.) Research advances have a way of snowballing. Scientists learn from failures and try new things. Suddenly, it seems like there are multiple promising agents for ALS—but this development only seems sudden to those observing from a distance. To Merit and other ALS clinicians and their patients, it seems like maybe, just maybe, an effective therapy will come just in time. She was a magnet for patients and a magnet for companies with new treatments to try, so once again, she is at the shared front line of patient care and research.

"It feels like change is in the air," she says. "There are so many people now studying this illness and so many new ideas. It feels like it's around the corner. Our job is to keep people as healthy as possible while these treatments are being developed."

Merit spends more than half her time in care or research for people with ALS. Remember the SOD1 mutation that Susan and her siblings had? Recalling the promise that she made to Susan in 1995, she says, "I'm excited to say that I really believe that I can keep that promise now. We are at the stage where we can give treatments to people that silence the genes like the one Susan had—and, in fact, we are doing those trials now."

At one time, ALS experts thought the problem was a loss of function of the gene, and tried infusing SOD1. That didn't work. "It became obvious that there was some toxic function caused by the mutation," Merit says. "If we could lower the amount of SOD1, at least in animal models, that could be curative. We needed to get to the point where we could unravel this, and we didn't get there until 2010."

A different treatment approach (called an antisense oligonucleotide treatment) was now possible. Merit designed a clinical trial, and when the trial was launched, she invited Susan's husband, whom she had kept in touch with. He was by then a colonel; Susan's son is in the military as well.

"He launched our investigator meeting," Merit says. "It was just incredibly powerful having him talk about the illness and its impact."

That trial showed that the antisense oligonucleotide seemed to be safe in humans, but in the meantime, some evidence of toxicity had emerged in monkeys and rats. (This was one of the three big disappointments for Merit in 2012.) So researchers went to work to redesign the treatment. It has taken four years, and the initial trial data with the newer agent are just becoming available.

"It takes persistence to do this kind of work," she says. "It's a long haul."

Despite the risk for burnout, the ALS team at the Healey Center has been amazingly stable, with little turnover. "Most people never leave ALS once they come into the field," Merit says. "We all share the same passion and drive. So our team has been together more than a decade, and we know each other as friends and colleagues."

She remains realistic but upbeat. "I really do love everything I do, and I believe that we can make a difference and defeat this illness," she says. "I've never been one to give up. Yes, it's a sad disease. There are days when I truly hate ALS. But I love my patients, and I love what we're doing. I feel that we are going to make a difference, and that sustains me and all our team."

CHAPTER

4 | Minimizing Fear

THE
GOOD
DOCTOR

LIKE MOST GOOD IDEAS, the goal of redesigning breast imaging to minimize fear for patients and their families did not come out of the blue. Nor did it take shape all at once. The pieces came together over a few years; only in retrospect does it seem the obvious thing to do.

From the start of her career as a breast radiologist, Emily Sedgwick had been troubled by the difference between the care received by most people and care received by a physician or a physician's family member. "When a woman has an abnormal mammogram, she finds out after she has gone home," Emily says. "And she usually has a biopsy sometime in the next several days. As any woman who has been through this process can tell you, even when the wait is only overnight, that night is a long one."

Emily couldn't help but notice that things were different when the patient was someone with whom the caregivers identified, like a doctor or a doctor's wife. The woman didn't leave. The biopsy was done right away. "The difference in the amount and the duration of fear and uncertainty that they faced compared with women who had routine care was, well, embarrassing," she says.

Most people deal with that kind of embarrassment by shrugging it off. Clinicians with self-awareness know there are those brief moments when one pauses, aware that things *could* be done differently to make the ensuing events smoother, quicker, less anxiety- provoking. But it's very easy to rationalize usual care by thinking about how giving everyone expedited care would disrupt everything. Colleagues would have to interrupt what they were doing and extend themselves in other ways. Other patients would have to wait if standard workflows are ignored. So, all too often, we let those moments pass and say things like, "We can book you for your breast biopsy on Monday."

The notion that there might be a better way to do things began to take shape when a technologist working with Emily suggested that they change how patients were scheduled. Emily realized that if her team began their day with the mammograms ordered for women who had abnormal breast exams, and who were thus more likely to need a biopsy, they could do more biopsies the same day.

That made Emily wonder, "What would it be like if my colleagues and I could treat everyone the way we would want to be treated—if everyone who needed a biopsy could have it the same day?"

The opportunity to realize this vision came in 2007, when Baylor College of Medicine (BCM) offered Emily a job. Local healthcare politics had caused BCM to start its own clinical programs. Some of those programs were not doing well in the highly competitive Houston healthcare environment. Breast imaging was one of them, and BCM asked Emily if she would leave her private practice to direct BCM's program.

"I think they were desperate," Emily recalls. Emily said she would come if they let her redesign the program the way she thought breast cancer screening should be done. They said yes, and she joined BCM a few months later, in July 2007.

Almost immediately, Baylor College of Medicine became one of the few places in the United States in which almost all women whose mammograms indicate they need a core needle biopsy get that procedure the same day.

* * *

To appreciate the care delivered by Emily and her team at BCM, it helps to understand how breast cancer screening works at most institutions. In general, women who have a mammogram return home after the images are taken. If the initial mammogram shows something abnormal, the women are called by their referring clinician and return for additional imaging on another day.

Screening mammograms are images obtained every year or two for women over age 40 who have no clinical evidence of breast abnormalities. Diagnostic mammograms are studies performed on women who either have an abnormality detected on physical examination, or have had an abnormal screening mammogram. Extra views are taken to get a more thorough look at the possible abnormality, and in about half of cases, ultrasound is used to further characterize it. If the additional studies are abnormal, a biopsy is recommended.

At many institutions, most of the biopsies are done within a day or two. An informal industry standard is that the biopsies should be done within a week of an abnormal mammogram. In healthcare delivery systems that do not work well, that interval can be much longer—months rather than days.

In BCM's breast cancer screening program and a small number of others around the country, that interval is reduced to hours. Core needle biopsies are performed in 95 percent of patients on the day they learn they need one. Most of them get the news within a day or two that the pathology results were negative, and they do not have cancer. If follow-up care is needed, they are given referrals.

That's not the only feature that makes Emily's program different. When she first started the same-day biopsy program at BCM, she convened a group of doctors, technicians, and administrators, and created standardized, evidence-based imaging protocols with the specific goal of reducing the number of times a woman goes in and out of the mammography room. The reason: when patients get called back into the room for more images, it causes a surge of anxiety. Now, at BCM, women are rarely summoned back into the room for further imaging. There is a modest decrease in "productivity" because BCM radiologists speak to every patient—even those undergoing just routine screening. But this approach decreases fear.

Why doesn't every organization do mammography this way? To make this work, the BMC team needed to be flexible—after all, on some days, no biopsies are necessary, but on other days, there might be seven. Emily tells her staff, "Everyone gets to eat their lunch every day—but it might not be at lunchtime."

The staff doesn't seem to mind. In fact, they seem to take pride in being flexible as individuals and as a group, so that women and their families have fewer sleepless nights wondering whether they have breast cancer.

* * *

Emily Sedgwick was born in Illinois in 1969, the first of three children of parents who came from families of modest means. Her father was raised on a farm in Raymond, Ohio, with six children in a two-bedroom house and an outhouse. Her mother was from a Kentucky coal-mining family, which eventually moved to Ohio. "My parents worked hard, and they both went to college at Ohio State University," Emily says. "My mother's college roommate was dating my dad's cousin, and they set them up on a blind date."

After Emily's parents married, they moved to Illinois, where Emily's father worked in construction, and Emily and her sister were born. After a couple of years in Illinois, the family moved back to Ohio because Emily's grandfather, a bricklayer, had had a heart attack and needed Emily's father in the family business.

Emily's father became a general contractor, and in 1979, they moved to California where he worked building restaurants for Rax Roast Beef, a fast-food chain. Another child, a son, came along. Emily's mother was a school teacher, but when the children started to arrive, she stayed home.

When Emily is asked about the origins of her breast-cancer-screening program, she starts by describing her parents and the values they conveyed. "My parents demanded that we demonstrate respect for every person that we knew," she recalls. "When I answered the phone, I had to say, 'Sedgwick residence—Emily speaking.' I had to call every adult 'Mister' or 'Mrs.' or 'Doctor.'"

Emily graduated from Bella Vista High School in Sacramento in 1988, where her initial plan had been to become a lawyer. "Those were the years of the TV show *LA Law*," she recalls. But a boyfriend's father thought medicine was a better career and introduced her to a pediatrician. "I followed that pediatrician around, and thought, 'I like this. I think I'll do medicine,'" she recalls. She broke up with that boyfriend, but stuck with the goal of becoming a doctor.

Emily had another goal during high school—to go to the University of California, Berkeley. Her sixth-grade teacher had gone to Berkeley and later had gotten a PhD at the University of Chicago. Eventually, he became faculty at Harvard and the Brookings Institution. "I thought he was the greatest thing ever," Emily recalls. "He was smart and treated us like we were adults. We talked about things that I didn't think 12-year-olds talked about. And he had gone to Berkeley, so that was always my goal, too."

She loved Berkeley. She knew she wanted to go to medical school, but she majored in history because she realized that this was her one chance to study something other than the sciences. She wrote her thesis on how lesbian-headed households had been influenced by the civil rights and women's rights movements.

Emily began to hone her political skills—skills that would come in useful when she began to redesign breast imaging at BCM—when she ran for a seat in the student senate. "There's nothing like campaigning to be elected—having to express your ideas to a bunch of people who vehemently disagree with you and figuring out how to engage them," she says.

Emily traces her progressive inclinations to her parents' message that she should be open-minded and always respect others—themes that resonated well with the culture at Berkeley. Berkeley's culture conveyed another value to young Emily, who says, "There was a powerful message that you should be willing to question the status quo."

The combination of these values became Emily's secret sauce. "I question the status quo, but I try to do it in a way that is respectful."

* * *

After graduation from Berkeley, Emily went directly to medical school at the University of California, San Francisco (UCSF). As before, she loved school, and she participated in student government. And as before, she found herself restless, wanting to take an active role in making something better.

It was a special time to be a medical student at UCSF. This was the period right before highly active antiretroviral therapy (HAART) turned HIV from a death sentence to a controllable disease. Before HAART came along, hospitals everywhere were filled with patients dying from AIDS, but nowhere in the United States was the suffering caused by epidemic more obvious than San Francisco.

"They were dying right and left," she recalls. "I mean . . . it seemed criminal."

Emily decided that she would go into surgery. "I wanted to fix things," she says. She matched at one of the top programs in the country, Brigham and Women's Hospital, and moved to Boston.

It was not an easy year or a happy one. Surgery was a male-dominated culture, and while Emily liked surgery itself, she decided she enjoyed her relationships with the trainees in radiology and switched to the Brigham's radiology program. Shortly after starting radiology training she decided to focus on breast radiology. She liked interacting with the women patients and helping them understand the complex set of decisions that flow from having an abnormal mammogram.

So after fits and starts, she had found her professional calling. And at the same time, she found her husband.

* * *

David Aguilar started his internship at the same time as Emily. They first met in the intensive care unit, where David was taking care of a patient who needed a urologic procedure. Emily was the intern on the urology service, and she and David had a nice conversation as she took care of the patient. It was the beginning of a casual friendship that came to life only when they happened to run into each other in the hospital.

Two years later, though, after they had both been assigned to work in the emergency department at the same time, Emily found herself thinking about David. She had dated other men, but nothing had felt right. "I asked myself, 'Who is the nicest person I know?'" she recalls. "And I thought, 'David Aguilar.' I promised myself that the next time I saw him, I would ask him out."

Less than a week later, on a rainy day in June 1998, Emily was walking to work, and a beat-up 1988 Chevy Nova pulled over near her. It was David Aguilar, asking if she wanted a ride to the hospital, which was only two blocks away.

"I thought God was telling me, 'This is the guy!'" she recalls. "I asked him out before I even put on my seat belt."

* * *

Emily knew she was going to marry him after their first date, which was supposed to be sailing on the Charles River on July 5. Emily was chief resident, and because the interns were so new in their roles, she had worked all night on July 4. Their plans for sailing were ruined by heavy rain. Instead they went out for breakfast at Johnny's, a popular "greasy spoon" restaurant in Newton, Massachusetts. She had some dates planned with other men, but she came home from breakfast and cancelled them.

She and David married on September 30, 2000. They had a son in January 2002, and a daughter 17 months later. While David finished his cardiology training at the Brigham, Emily worked in a practice outside Boston for a year. They began to think about where they should settle down, and moving close to Aguilar's parents had obvious appeal.

David was from Pasadena, Texas. His mother had come to the United States from Mexico as an undocumented immigrant in her teen years and had been deported. She returned legally when she was in her twenties and met David's father. He was also of Mexican heritage, but had been born in El Paso. Neither parent graduated from high school, although David's father got his GED. All three of their children went to medical school, and all three married other physicians.

Emily and David moved with their two young children to Houston in 2003. David, who had gone to Baylor College of Medicine, joined the faculty there and soon moved into a role combining clinical care with research in diabetes and heart failure. Emily started working for a large private practice that provided radiology services to another hospital at Texas Medical Center.

And that is where she was in 2007, when BCM came calling, and she took the new role with the goal of redesigning how breast cancer imaging is done.

* * *

"Although the idea of same-day biopsies is simple, it wasn't as easy as it might sound," Emily says. Indeed, two barriers still keep most institutions from doing breast cancer screening this way.

The most obvious show-stopper is financial. Radiologists can read more mammograms per hour if they are in a room looking at one image after another. The imaging equipment is used more efficiently if patients shuttle in and out of the room and are called back in if they need further studies.

In BCM's program, however, the women usually remain in the room until a radiologist has looked at the images. That way, they don't have to experience the surge of fear that is so common when women are told their initial images are potentially abnormal. This approach does hurt BMC's "productivity" per physician, which runs at about the 35th to 40th percentile of breast cancer screening programs. Nevertheless, the program itself has grown, as same-day care is attractive to patients and referring physicians. As a result, BCM enjoys the financial rewards from having more clinical breast cancer business. But radiologists seeking to maximize their incomes could probably do better elsewhere.

The other major barrier is the unpredictability of the number of biopsies needed on any given day. Doing an ultrasound- guided biopsy takes Emily about four minutes, but the entire process of setting up the room, getting informed consent, and so on, takes about an hour. The procedure/imaging room is tied up for about 30 minutes. The challenge of creating and managing a program that might have no biopsies one day and seven the next was not something Emily had learned about in her clinical training. It took a combination of leadership and management skills that Emily had to acquire as she went along.

* * *

Leadership begins with a clear idea of what one is trying to accomplish, and Emily came to this work with strongly held values. She was not shy about expressing them, but not overbearing either. She attracted colleagues who shared those values and who felt proud to be associated with them.

When she looks back on why she started this work in 2007—at a time when her children were toddlers, she and her husband were relatively inexperienced physicians, and life felt a little out-of-control in general—she says, "I had this feeling that there *is* such a thing as right and wrong. When patients aren't treated well, it really makes me mad. I needed to be able to channel that anger in a way that was productive. I thought, 'Here I am in the breast center. What can I do to make it less terrifying?'"

The message from Emily's parents about respecting others helped her build enduring relationships with her colleagues, including the nonphysicians. "I listened to my team," she says, as she recalls how the idea of same-day biopsies took shape before BCM approached her. "I remember sitting in the reading room, and one of the technologists was talking about how she thought we should do the diagnostic imaging in the morning because that's when the doctors and the technologists are at their best. I thought, "Gosh, if I do my diagnostic exams—the ones who are most likely to need a biopsy—in the mornings, then it gives me the flexibility to do the biopsies in the afternoon."

When Emily became the director of breast imaging at BCM in 2007, she recruited some of the technologists who had worked with her in her private practice. "We liked each other," she says. "But they also were interested. They believed in the idea of doing biopsies the same day. Several are still here."

* * *

Still, the challenges were daunting. BCM had just one other breast radiologist, and within six months he decided to leave. Emily was still fresh from training as a clinician and was not trained to be an administrator or a manager. She had become the director of a two-physician group—and now one of those physicians had left. Emily was reading every breast image herself.

"I was so naïve, and I really didn't understand how much went into it," she says. "You need to think about compliance, engaging referring physicians, cross-training technologists, and firing people who aren't committed to the cause."

Believing in "the cause" of reducing unnecessary fear for women undergoing breast cancer screening was critical, because Emily was asking a lot of her colleagues. They had to make flexibility part of their normal way of doing business—not just something they summoned when a special patient might benefit from expedited care. This is what students of management call resilience thinking—building systems that show their strengths when the unexpected arises.

To do that, Emily needed team members whose personal sense of self is so intertwined with the goal that they will do what it takes to meet it. That might mean delaying their lunch on some days or even missing it. It means cross-training personnel so that when something needs to be done, there is more than one person around who can do it.

Emily picked up management skills from a range of short-term courses and learned to standardize work in ways that reduced rework and waste. As suggested by her technologist, they scheduled women who are more likely to require breast biopsies in the morning, giving the team more time later in the day for procedures, if needed.

Today, all breast radiologists (there are seven) share the same skills and use standardized reporting approaches. Every mammographic technologist can perform biopsies, which increases the chances that women will have all of their care from one technologist—a step that Emily hopes can reduce anxiety, since the patient and technologist may already have a bond.

Emily has given attention to "soft" skills, too—particularly early and frequent communication with patients. Because management protocols are standardized, technologists can communicate with patients with confidence about next steps and wait times. Radiologists talking to patients about biopsies have those conversations when the patient is clothed and sitting at eye level with the doctor. The radiologists have standardized their communication approaches in ways that ease patients' fears but also are clear. Once the biopsy results come back from pathology, the findings are communicated to patients by the next available radiologist, rather than awaiting the return of the radiologist who originally talked to the patient.

Emily had to do more than develop the same-day biopsy program. She started a breast MRI program and an MRI-guided biopsy program at the same time.

She realized that fewer than 10 percent of radiologists are breast-imaging experts—and knew that experience really mattered. Radiologists who were focused upon breast imaging did a better job detecting disease, while also putting fewer women through unnecessary biopsies. "So I realized that I needed to start a training program. I wanted to grow our program, and I wasn't going to be able to do that unless I started training people. So I applied for a breast-imaging fellowship program, and our first fellow started in 2010."

She even took to the road to talk to referring physicians. Equipped with a PowerPoint presentation she had created, she went to meetings of ob-gyns, family practice physicians, and general internal medicine groups. She told referring physicians that they could send over women with breast complaints for a same-day evaluation, without any appointment.

She started a continuing medical education (CME) program on breast cancer care for the primary care physician and scheduled it for September. One colleague said, "You don't want to have a course during hurricane season."

"I laughed to myself and thought that's never going to happen," she recalls. "Of course, on the exact day my course was supposed to begin, we had a hurricane. I cancelled it, and put it on later."

* * *

Emily was proud of how breast imaging changed at BCM in her first few years as director, but she was aware that a few miles away, thousands of women had to wait weeks for follow-up of an abnormal mammogram—if they had mammograms at all. Harris Health System is the county government-sponsored program that provides medical care for the estimated 30 percent of adults who are uninsured in Houston. Emily learned that median time between a woman learning she had abnormal results on screening mammography and having an image-guided core-needle breast biopsy was 89 days. The median time between abnormal mammogram results and the first day of treatment was 121 days.

The problem at Harris Health wasn't sleepless nights. It was sleepless months.

Again, chance created an opportunity for Emily to make a difference. Her care had won the appreciation of many patients and their families—and some of those patients were wealthy and made substantial donations to BCM. (One donor funded the Pat Korell Endowed Professorship in Breast Imaging, which supported Emily's salary.)

An oil executive, Lester Smith, had become a supporter of BCM as he went through the loss of his first wife and other relatives to breast cancer. One day, he came to see Emily. He told her that he was thinking of making a gift to Harris Health, and he had an idea of what he hoped would result.

"I want you to go give those ladies over there the same kind of care that you give here," he said. Emily said she would, and Smith wrote a check to Harris Health for $15 million. The contribution wasn't tied to any particular building or programmatic initiatives. He was basically nudging Emily, and he did not need to push hard.

The CEO at Harris Health was also ready to work with her. His wife had been Emily's patient, and he understood the same-day model. So when Emily started spending a day a week at Harris Health, the high-level support was already there for breaking down traditional obstacles and streamlining care.

She started working at Harris Health in 2011, leading the BCM-associated programs in breast cancer screening, and opened the Smith Clinic in 2012. The year Emily started, Harris Health was performing about 12,000 mammograms per year at various clinical sites, including the mobile mammography van. Soon, the number had risen to 48,000 per year.

That 89-day interval between abnormal mammogram and core needle biopsy? Within 18 months, Harris Health was offering same-day biopsies to women who came to the central diagnostic center. Many women would have an initial screening mammogram at one of the dozen community sites, but patients at high-risk or those with abnormal initial studies would undergo imaging at that central center. Emily and her colleagues quickly learned that they couldn't make the interval too short between the initial mammogram at a community site and the diagnostic study at the central location. "These women don't have cars," she says. "They don't have child care. About 70 percent of the people who go to Harris Health are employed, but they are hourly workers, and they need to make accommodations in order to take the time and come in."

In response, Emily and her colleagues targeted a 14-day interval for getting biopsies done for women who had had abnormal screening mammograms. By 2015, Harris Health had had an 89 percent improvement in time from abnormal results on screening mammography to biopsy, and a 67 percent improvement in time to first day of treatment.

* * *

Emily did not begin this work in search of fame or power. She started because she was indignant about the discrepancy between how most patients were treated and how she and her colleagues knew it should be done. But her work has not gone unnoticed at BCM and across the country. In 2016, BCM made her chief quality officer, and asked her to start improving care on a broader basis. And toward the end of 2018, she was recruited to be chief medical officer at a major Houston hospital run by the national hospital system, HCA.

In the breast cancer-screening world, her name is well known and her program much admired—even if not nearly as widely imitated as she would like. BCM's breast cancer screening program now has 6.6 FTE breast radiologists. This growth does not reflect expansion of Houston's population; as BCM's business has gone up, others' business has gone down. Patients and referring physicians send their patients to BCM because they are relieved to have the results on the same day, and they have spread the word about BCM's breast cancer screening among their friends and colleagues. Patient-experience scores rank above the 97th percentile.

Emily understands that going where she was really needed— BCM at a time of crisis—helped create the opportunity to shape care. "There's no way I could have done everything I've done if I was working at a larger institution.

"The same-day program does not conform to the traditional metrics for productivity. If we were sitting in a dark room somewhere with the door closed, we would certainly crank out more mammograms," she says. "But the patients would be paying the price in terms of anxiety and wait. Because we are face-to-face with patients, we are unable to realize the same levels of productivity. But we've been able to make the case with our leadership based on market analysis. We have demonstrated that our volume has been able to grow in our highly competitive market."

Asked about her proudest moment, she responds: "I was in an elevator, and a woman recognized me as the person who had diagnosed her with her breast cancer in the remote past. She looked at me, and said, 'You know it was such a horrible experience, but what you and your team did was by far the best part of the whole thing, and I am so grateful for how you handled it.'

"That really was my whole objective," Emily continues. "To make something a little less horrible in an overall tragic experience."

* * *

A few days after my long conversation with Emily about her work, she sent me an email with one final thought. She had been thinking about the impact of her parents again, and she wrote, "My mom taught me to leave a place better than I found it. She told me that as I left for my first babysitting gig when I was 12. It's a philosophy that's played out in both my personal and professional lives."

CHAPTER 5

THE GOOD DOCTOR

Fighting the Root Cause

JOSEPH SAKRAN WAS EXHAUSTED. It was the evening of November 7, 2018, and the 41-year-old trauma surgeon had just gotten home after a long day in the operating room at Johns Hopkins. He was unwinding by sitting on the couch in his living room, eating dinner, and like so many of his generation, simultaneously taking in information from a variety of sources. While the television played in the background, he scanned magazines and medical journals, and periodically looked at his iPhone to see what was new on Twitter.

Then he saw something on Twitter that gave him pause. Someone had written that the National Rifle Association (NRA) had tweeted a comment about how doctors should not take positions on gun control and that they should "stay in their lane."

Sakran had seen plenty on Twitter with no basis in fact, so he went to the NRA's Twitter messages. The NRA had indeed sent out a tweet at 2:43 p.m. that afternoon that said, "Someone should tell self-important anti-gun doctors to stay in their lane. Half of the articles in Annals of Internal Medicine are pushing for gun control. Most upsetting, however, the medical community seems to have consulted *no one* but themselves."

The NRA tweet was in response to a series of articles that had just been published in the highly respected medical journal *Annals of Internal Medicine*. The articles had documented the relationship between stringent gun laws and lower firearm death rates, and included an editorial calling for physicians to speak out on gun violence as a public health issue. Sakran didn't expect the NRA to like the idea of a medical journal adding its voice to the coalition pushing for gun control, but something about the phrase "stay in their lane" got to him.

Sakran is director of emergency general surgery at Johns Hopkins Hospital, which sits on the edge of the neighborhoods featured in the television show *The Wire*. As a result, Sakran sees gunshot victims all the time; many he helps save, but some he cannot. It's emotionally draining work, the kind that causes burnout in many doctors and nurses. The idea that someone should say physicians like him were "self-important" and tell them, basically, to shut up. . . .

"I was incensed," he said.

He immediately tweeted back: "As a Trauma Surgeon and survivor of #GunViolence I cannot believe the audacity of the @NRA to make such a divisive statement. We take care of these patients every day. Where are you when I'm having to tell all those families their loved one has died. @DocsDemand #Docs4GunSense."

As events would soon show, the NRA tweet could not have come at a worse time. Only a few hours later, 13 people were killed in yet another mass shooting at the Borderline Bar and Grill, a country-and-western bar that was a favorite hangout of college students in Thousand Oaks, California. The NRA tweet led to more than 22,000 comments, most of them critical, many from physicians who, like Sakran, saw the NRA tweet as adding an outrageous insult to horrible injuries.

In the days that followed, Sakran could not put the NRA tweet out of his mind. He created a Twitter platform with the "handle" @ThisIsOurLane. Its description is "Medical Professionals who care for #GunViolence Victims. We are 'in our lane' when we propose solutions to prevent Firearm Injury and Death. #ThisIsOurLane."

He added in a tweet "Since the @NRA is incapable of understanding the important role we the medical community have in this fight against #GunViolence, we have created this handle just for you!"

He glanced a few hours later and saw that there were already 500 followers. The next day, he saw there were 7,000, and soon @ThisIsOurLane had gone viral. As of April 2019, there are more than 29,000 followers. Physicians, nurse, and other healthcare professionals sent in stories and photos of blood on the floors and walls of the trauma bays and operating rooms after frantic efforts to save gunshot wound victims. A resident physician sent in a photo of his bloodstained scrubs, and wrote "First patient, first day of residency: gunshot wound to the head. Tried saving him as his mother cried into my shoulder pleading for us to save him. He didn't make it. He wasn't the last one either. #ThisIsMyLane #ThisIsOurLane #NRA."

Another physician wrote: "Single GSW [gun shot wound] to the head as a drive-by. Surprising little blood, but plenty of blood-curdling screams from this middle schooler's mother when we told her that her baby was dead. Tell me @NRA how do I get her screams out of my head 4 years later? #ThisIsMyLane #GunControlNow."

Yet another showed his blood-soaked pants legs, and wrote "Can't post a patient photo . . . so this is a selfie. This is what it looks like to #stayinmylane. @NRA @JosephSakran."

#ThisIsOurLane had caught on. Sakran had sounded just the right note of indignation, with the voice of experience of a clinician who actually cared for gunshot victims and consoled their families. The media starting writing stories about Sakran and the movement he had helped set in motion. The *New York Times* ran a front page story. The *New England Journal of Medicine* ran a perspective piece at the front of an issue, saying in part: "#ThisIsOurLane calls attention to the role of physicians from many walks of medical life—trauma surgery, emergency medicine, radiology, anesthesiology, surgery, physical medicine, rehabilitation, psychiatry, and forensic pathology. It encompasses our colleagues as well: paramedics who face carnage in the field, nurses who provide massive transfusions, housekeeping staff who clean blood-soaked floors, pharmacists who assist with intensive care unit (ICU) medication dosing, and everyone who helps survivors piece their lives back together and helps families recover from loss. This is their lane, too."[8]

The *Washington Post* ran a long story on Sakran on November 14. National Public Radio's legendary interviewer Terry Gross broadcast a 37-minute interview with Sakran on November 28.

The flurry of attention made Sakran something of a celebrity. FierceHealthcare named him one of five physicians to watch in the year ahead. He was seen as akin to the news anchor who becomes unhinged in the movie *Network* and starts a movement by yelling, "We're mad as hell, and we're not going to take it." Sakran was asked to speak around the country and write essays for magazines.

Asked about this public response, Sakran shrugged and said that he was just a physician taking care of patients who were all too often victims of gun violence. It was reasonable to assume that almost any doctor or other healthcare personnel would have been upset, he said, and he pointed out repeatedly that many of the followers of @ThisIsOurLane are gun owners as well as healthcare providers.

But the fact is that Sakran had more reason to care about gun violence than most physicians or other healthcare personnel.

When he was 17, he was shot in the throat in a random act of gun violence. He nearly died and had a tracheostomy for six months.

At an age when most teenagers are enjoying the last gasps of adolescence, he had what might have been his last gasps. That ordeal influenced his journey into medicine and how he feels about his work today—including those moments when he has to tell family members that one of their own has been gravely injured.

* * *

When asked where he is from, Joseph Sakran pauses, takes a deep breath, and says, "It's complicated." He starts with his parents, but quickly goes a generation further back. He explains that both of his parents are Lebanese, but they grew up in Israel and emigrated to the United States in the early 1970s. His family background explains why he speaks both Arabic and Hebrew, and has something to do with why he became a doctor, a trauma surgeon, and ultimately a leader in the campaign against gun violence.

Sakran's father, Victor Sakran, was born in Nazareth, where his Greek Orthodox ancestors lived long before it became part of Israel. Sakran's grandfather owned a small store in the center of town, right near "Mary's Well" (the site of the Annunciation, where, according to Catholic tradition, the Angel Gabriel appeared to Mary and told her that she would bear the son of God).

Sakran never knew this grandfather, but countless stories made his grandfather something of a role model. His grandfather had an enormous family (11 children, some of whom died in infancy) and an even larger circle of friends. He was not wealthy, but he was a religious man with a reputation for welcoming anyone into their home.

"I heard over and over growing up that my grandfather stood for selfless service," Sakran says. "He really tried to make the community better. I've been back to visit, and all the information I have is that he was someone who led by example. He was the same even when no one was looking. My parents gave me a very clear message as I grew up that behaving this way was part of what it meant to be in our family."

Sakran's father came to the United States in the early 1960s, following an older brother who had moved to Miami. "My dad came with just a quarter in his pocket—literally, nothing," Sakran says. "But he worked hard and put himself through school. He was living in the basement of his brother's home. He wanted to become a doctor, but he didn't have the means or opportunity. But he became an aerodynamic engineer and ended up working for Cessna focusing on both commercial and military projects."

Victor Sakran's work took him to Wichita, Kansas, but then he was recruited for a position in the US Department of Commerce and moved to northern Virginia, just outside Washington, DC. Meanwhile, he had met the young woman by the name of Nuhad, who would become his wife. Nuhad was a friend of his sister, the only child of a Syrian-Lebanese-Catholic couple that had decided to move to Haifa, Israel, and run a small store. Nuhad and Victor met, they married, and they moved to the United States.

In 1977, they had the first of three children, Joseph, who was born on August 3, 1977, at Inova Fairfax Hospital in Falls Church, Virginia. Two years later, a daughter, Jennifer, was born. And two years after that, they had a third child, another son named Mark.

* * *

For the first 17 years of Joe Sakran's life, his family's experience was a classic American immigrant success story. He remembers his father getting up every day at 5 a.m. to go to work, and his mother staying home to take care of the children, but then going back to work as a teacher. "They faced their share of adversity," he says. "They had accents, and people were always asking where they were from. I think back then it was more the lack of diversity that existed rather than hatred. But it wasn't easy.

"I would say that my parents were *really* involved in our upbringing," he says. "They felt that nothing was more important than education—that it was the path to success. So we played sports, we played musical instruments, we had friends—but nothing was more important than our educations. In the summer, we didn't just bolt out the door and play the whole day. We had to read book chapters and then summarize what we had read."

Joe Sakran did not seek his first job until he was 17. "My father always said that *his* job as a parent was to go to work and make ends meet," he recalls. "My job was to get educated. That was my responsibility."

It was only when he began his senior year at the local public school, Lake Braddock Secondary School in Burke, Virginia, that he signed on for part-time work at a pet store. He was supposed to start on Saturday, September 24, 1994, at noon.

He never got there. At that moment, he was regaining consciousness in the ICU of the hospital in which he had been born.

* * *

The evening before, Sakran and almost everyone else he knew had gone to the first football game of the season for his high school. He had had a busy afternoon, going from school to an SAT preparation class that his parents had enrolled him in. He got home from that class, and one of his friends was already waiting for him. He barely had time to drop his things off and change. "My parents were trying to ask me how my class had been," he remembers. "I said, 'I'll tell you later, I have to go.' And I ran out of the house."

He went to the game, and afterward, Sakran joined a group of his friends. "We were just chatting it up," he says. "But at a nearby park, a fight had broken out between two individuals. One pulled out a gun and started firing. I got hit by a random bullet.

"The experience is still very clear in my mind, but it's also very fuzzy in the sense that it happened so quickly," he says.

"I remember that I heard people yell, and I remember turning to my right and seeing flashes. Then I felt numb. I wasn't sure what had happened, but I knew something wasn't right. It seemed like the group around me was disbursing in slow motion."

At this point, Sakran was still on his feet, and he walked to the curb of street. He could not talk. A .38 caliber bullet had entered the front side of his throat, ruptured his trachea (windpipe), nicked his left carotid artery, exited his neck, and lodged in his left shoulder. Blood was streaming from the artery. He could only mouth words and nod his head to answer yes or no.

"I was wearing a white shirt, and I was just drenched in blood," he says. "A couple of my friends saw me, and they were trying to figure out where I had been shot. They tried to lay me down, and when they did, I started choking on blood."

Someone stopped a car, and asked the driver to call 911. The police medevac helicopter arrived before conventional ground ambulances, but Sakran could not be transported by air. The small chopper could only accommodate patients who could lie supine, and he could not, because his airway quickly would fill with blood. Within minutes an ambulance arrived. Emergency medical technicians (EMTs) started an intravenous line and took him to Inova Fairfax Hospital.

In the trauma center at Inova Fairfax Hospital, Sakran was surrounded by the trauma team of physicians, nurses, and other staff. The trauma surgeon had not arrived yet. Sakran could tell that there was disagreement among the team about what to do next. He even overheard a discussion between the emergency department physician and the trauma resident: "I'm not going to get sued if we lose him."

At that point, the trauma surgeon, Robert Ahmed, arrived, noticed the chaos, and immediately took charge. Sakran's memory is that Ahmed said, "What in the fuck are you all doing?" Ahmed said Sakran had to go the operating room immediately, unlocked the gurney, and began wheeling him toward the operating room. Once there, Ahmed laid Sakran flat—a challenge, because Sakran was still choking on his blood when he leaned backward. Ahmed looked down at Sakran and said, "I'm sorry, but I have to do this to save your life." That was the last thing Sakran remembers before passing out.

Ahmed and the surgical team did an emergency tracheostomy and explorations of both sides of his neck. During the explorations they found significant damage to the left carotid artery. Dipankar Mukherjee, the vascular surgeon on call, took a piece of Sakran's saphenous vein (from his leg) and created a patch to repair the hole in the artery. An ear, nose, and throat specialist, Timothy McBride, worked on reconstructing his trachea.

Sakran woke up the next day in the ICU. He could not talk or really move. For the next two days, his breathing was performed by a ventilator connected to his lungs through his tracheostomy. He stared straight ahead and saw a clock on the wall. When he woke up it was almost noon—the time that he was supposed to start his new job, his first job, at the pet store. He remembers thinking, "Oh, shit! I'm going to be late."

And then he saw his family around him. Both of his parents were there, along with his sister, his brother, and his mother's father, who was living with them at the time. They were horrified. "I could see from the looks on their faces that what had happened was really bad," he says. "They had worried so much about me and my brother and sister, but I don't think they could have ever imagined that something like this might happen."

Sakran often thinks about what his family went through that day. "Now when parents or other family members get called to come to the hospital because their loved one has been hurt, it's hard not to see my own family in their place," he says. "Sometimes, when I go out to talk to families, I tell them that things can turn out fine—my own story is proof of that. But that's not always the case. Sometimes, I look at these families, and I have to tell them that their loved one is never coming home again. And their lives are never the same."

* * *

Sakran's road to recovery was a long one. He was in the hospital for a little over a month and went home with his tracheostomy tube, which stayed in place for six months. During that period, he had several follow-up operations to remove scar tissue that resulted from his body's attempt to repair the damage. They were necessary to prevent the narrowing of his trachea. He had a paralyzed left vocal cord, and to this day, his voice gets hoarse when he is tired. He also lost function of his left phrenic nerve, the nerve that tells the diaphragm (the sheet of muscle between the lungs and abdomen) to contract, and thus enlarge the chest and pull air into the lungs. His chest x-ray today shows his left diaphragm frozen high in his chest.

He was damaged, but he wasn't dead—and he was still a high school student who wanted to graduate with his classmates. His school and local county government rose to the occasion and provided home schooling, which enabled him to catch up and then keep up with his classmates. In the spring, he returned to school. He graduated with his class.

But before that graduation, before his tracheostomy came out, there was a defining moment. He was standing in the bathroom, looking in the mirror, taking in all the scars and other vestiges of his ordeal. He was down. "This is horrible," he remembers thinking. "What did I do to deserve this?"

At that moment, his father walked by. He could see the expression on his son's face in the mirror, and understood what was happening.

"Listen," his father said. "What happened to you is terrible. But you have a couple of options. One is that you can feel sorry for yourself. The other is that you can take this terrible tragedy, turn it into something positive, and use it to make a difference in the lives of other people."

"It was an 'uh-huh' moment," Sakran says. "I thought to myself, 'He's right. This sucks. But I have the possibility to do the best that I can to positively impact the lives of others.'"

* * *

Sakran started to think about becoming a doctor. He cannot really remember what he imagined himself doing before he was shot, but afterward he says, "I asked myself, 'What can I do that will allow me to give other people the same second chance I was given?'" He decided that he would try to go to medical school. Before long, he started to picture himself as a surgeon—a trauma surgeon operating on patients with injuries like the one he had had.

He wanted to stay close to home as his recovery continued, and applied to only one school—nearby George Mason University. He did really well academically in college—better than he had in high school before being shot. And he picked up some new skills that would enhance his ability to help people in danger. He became an EMT and a firefighter. He spent six months training as a firefighter, which occupied every Tuesday and Thursday evening and every weekend. Then he started responding to alarms and putting out fires.

"I loved it," he says. "It was exhilarating—it really is not like movies like *Backdraft*. It is so hot in those rooms that it is hard to describe. And when you walk out of there, there's a feeling that is hard to describe. You feel like you have *really* done something. My parents were really worried at one point that I loved being a firefighter so much that I wasn't going to go to medical school."

* * *

He did go to medical school, but not close to home—at least, not literally. Sakran went to Ben-Gurion University in Israel, his parents' home country. His parents had often talked about what an amazing place Israel was to live and go to school, and Ben-Gurion had a unique relationship with Columbia University. So the Medical School for International Health provided an ideal chance to get a medical education, get to know his extended family, learn a new language, and learn about life—all at the same time.

The experience was all he had hoped for. He learned medicine, came to know his relatives, and lived in a society at the nexus of Christianity, Judaism, and Islam. "Living in Jerusalem was just mind-blowing," he says. "I think I really developed as a person there."

He also learned how easily tolerance can give way to hate. He moved to Israel in the summer of 2000, and that fall, Ariel Sharon made his controversial visit to the Temple Mount—a provocative act that led to a period of Israeli-Palestinian violence known as the Second Intifada. As a student, he helped treat victims of suicide bombers in Jerusalem. "To hear some of the hatred that existed among both sides was hard," Sakran says. "But it's not the majority of what I heard. What you see on television is not representative of how people behave. For the most part, the Arabs and the Jews in Israel actually get along pretty well. You see that in a lot of different cities, like Jaffa and Haifa.

"Is there an analogy to tensions with the NRA?" he wonders. "I can't help but think that on a whole lot of issues, not just firearms, a problem in this country is that we just don't listen to each other. I guess I have had one useful lesson in life from my gunshot wound—I learned to deal with adversity. But another comes from living in the Middle East. I know we have to be willing to listen to each other in order to make progress on issues that affect our communities."

* * *

When it came time to apply for residency, Sakran's first choice was Inova Fairfax Hospital. Inova has a good general surgery training program, but not a famous one, and Sakran's friends asked him why he didn't rank other more traditional academic institutions, like Columbia, number one. Sakran had no ambivalence about the decision. He had been living overseas, and he wanted to come home for the next five years of his life, which could be difficult ones.

Inova was home. He had been born at Inova. He had nearly died at Inova. When he worked as an EMT during college, he had been based at Inova. He had rotated at Inova as a medical student. The two surgeons who played critical roles in treating him the night of his gunshot wound, Bob Ahmed and Dipankar Mukherjee, still worked there.

"I said to myself, what could be more inspiring than going back to Inova and training with the people who had saved my life?" he recalls.

"It was a tremendous experience. It was just wonderful to be physically close to my family" Sakran says. "Inova has a very comprehensive general surgical program that allowed me to develop my focus, and to develop the necessary skills to become a surgeon in the presence of the physicians and nurses who had saved my life. Sometimes, my hands would shake because I was so anxious to be the best I could be for them. I wanted to make them proud."

After surgical residency he spent two years at the Trauma Center at Penn Presbyterian Medical Center, part of the Hospital of University of Pennsylvania, doing a fellowship in traumatology and surgical critical care. Aside from deepening his expertise with the cardiovascular, infectious, and metabolic issues that often determine whether a traumatized patient recovers or dies after surgery, he had his first experiences as a teacher—one who would use his own story to bring insight to others.

The Trauma Center at Penn brought in high school students from underserved areas in the surrounding community. The program faculty asked Sakran to talk to them about gun violence and take them through the trauma center. They were primarily 14- to 15-year-old African American youths. Sakran would walk them through the facilities, and as would be expected of teenagers, many of the students would be distracted, giving Sakran less than their full attention.

But when he sat them in a room and told them the story of his gunshot wound—what it took to save him, and his long, difficult recovery—"all of their eyeballs would be completely focused on me," he says.

"I hadn't expected that," he says. "I said to myself, 'My gosh, what just happened?' And that's when I realized the power of my story. Until then, I had really thought, 'Who cares that I got shot?'"

Sakran always asked those students how many of them had been personally affected or knew someone who had been a victim of gun violence. Almost every hand would shoot up in answer. When Sakran told his story, he felt he was transitioning from just one more white guy in a white coat to someone who had insight into what they had been living with and fearing in their own communities.

His medical training and the work he did gave him credibility. But his history of being shot and surviving gave him relatability. He had gotten a glimpse of the power of telling one's story.

It was at this point that Sakran began to wonder, "I if I'm to follow the tradition of my grandfather in Nazareth—the one who did all he could for his community—should I try to do good on a larger scale?" He knew he wanted to be a trauma surgeon. He loved the work. He had a bit of the meticulousness and artistry he saw in his father, the engineer, and he could express those traits in the operating room. And just as he had felt when he worked as a firefighter or an EMT, as a surgeon he felt like he had *done something real* on a regular basis.

He decided that the logical next step in his career was to stop being a trainee and start being a real grown-up surgeon.

An opportunity came up at the Medical University of South Carolina, where Dr. Samir Fakhry, former chief of trauma surgery at Inova Fairfax Hospital, had taken a new role as division chief and recruited Sakran. When Sakran visited, he found Charleston beautiful and realized that it was just an hour flight away from his family. He took the job in 2012 and spent almost four years there.

It is clear in retrospect that well before Sakran arrived in Charleston, he had broader agendas on his mind. During medical school, he had taken a year off to get a masters of public health at Johns Hopkins, so he already had had some formal, big-picture education about health and healthcare. During medical school in Israel, he had helped take care of Bedouins in the desert and Black Hebrews from Dimona. After the Indian Ocean tsunami in 2004, he helped organize relief for the damaged city of Pondicherry, India, and in 2010 after the earthquake in Haiti, he also helped set up clinic services there. During his residency, he continued to work on developing healthcare interventions in low- and middle-income countries.

So it was no surprise that when he arrived in Charleston, he was made director of Global Disaster Preparedness for the Department of Surgery. And no surprise that after a few years, he sought permission to go to Harvard's Kennedy School of Government to get a masters of public administration to learn how to effect change on a larger scale. He took a large cut in his salary to sit in classrooms again, learning how political leaders think and exert influence. He learned about the power of social media and started a Doctors for Hillary grassroots movement. He became active on Facebook and Twitter.

It was also no surprise that by the end of his Kennedy School fellowship, he was offered other opportunities. Sakran didn't feel like he was an expert in public policy who had all the answers for what should happen. "What I realized was that I *was* a doctor, I really knew about issues that mattered to patients, and I was learning how to help patients by building relationships, bringing people together, and developing partnerships," he says. "I never wanted to stop being a trauma surgeon. I love that rush of taking care of patients, the way I loved the rush of being a firefighter. But I can't help but want to help patients on a larger scale, too. To me, it's the same work."

* * *

Sakran was recruited to be director of Emergency General Surgery and associate chief of the Division of Acute Care Surgery at Johns Hopkins Hospital. The job was attractive in so many ways, including being a short driving distance from his family. He has an elective general surgery practice, in which he performs routine general surgery (e.g., hernia, gallbladder, and colon surgery), often using robotic techniques. But he also takes care of trauma patients and cares for patients in the surgical critical care unit. Right before our first conversation, he had been in the operating room performing an emergency operation on a patient with a very low white blood count due to chemotherapy ("neutropenia") who had developed a perforation of the large intestine.

November 7, 2018, had also been an operating-room day for Sakran—a long day of being on his feet and concentrating for hours in a row. When he read the NRA tweet, his passionate response was spontaneous, visceral. "It's not like I took a long time to think about what I was going to say," he says. "I just responded back as someone who was online and taking care of his patients."

One of the details of the NRA tweet that bothered Sakran was the implication that physicians like himself had not tried to engage with the NRA in the past. He is, after all, an Arab-American who went to medical school in Israel and strongly believes that the world would be better if everyone would listen to the voices of those on the other side. Sakran notes that leadership from the American College of Surgeons *had* actually met with NRA leadership in January 2017, and expresses irritation that the NRA suggests that physician leadership has not attempted to find a reasonable middle ground.

In fact, just one week after the NRA tweet, a working group from the American College of Surgeons issued "middle ground" recommendations for gun-safety recommendations that included robust background checks, enhanced gun-safety training, mandatory reporting requirements for people considered being a threat to themselves or others, and use of innovative technologies to prevent accidental firing. The American College of Surgeons working group consisted of 22 authors, of whom 18 were gunowners.

But indignation over an inaccuracy in the NRA tweet was not what made Sakran's Twitter response resonate with so many clinicians. It was the implication that medical personnel had no role in attempting to reduce gun violence

"The worse part of my job is having to speak to families of patients who have been critically injured," he says. "We're able to save a lot of people, but we're not able to save everyone. Sometimes, when I go out to those waiting rooms, I look at those mothers and those fathers, and I realize that what I'm about to do is going to change their lives. I'm about to go out there and tell them that their loved one is never coming home again.

"That never gets easier," he says. "I often look at those faces, and I wonder what my parents thought when that surgeon came out to talk to them."

* * *

Starting #ThisIsOurLane was an effort by Sakran to give a strong voice to clinicians like himself and to help create a community for them. It was a blend of his experience as a clinician, what he learned at Harvard's Kennedy School of Government, and the zillion hours of his youth playing around on social media.

"My goal was to provide a platform to unite healthcare professionals, to have one strong voice in this fight to end gun violence in America," he says. "To my surprise, it exploded overnight. I think it showed that people were waiting to have this type of platform where they could express what they're seeing day in and day out within healthcare."

#ThisIsOurLane brought him a flurry of attention, invitations to speak, and even suggestions that he should consider running for public office. He sees public policy roles as natural outgrowths of being a clinician. "Being in the operating room and making one life-saving decision after another is incredibly gratifying," he says. "But when you do that day after day, you realize that you have both the possibility and the responsibility to work beyond the trauma center, beyond the operating room. There are clinicians across the spectrum who are so moved by what is taking place and want to be part of the solution as well. Frankly, a lot of the times, the best thing we can do in healthcare is prevention, and that is especially true for those of us who treat critically injured patients."

His personal story has made him an effective advocate for initiatives to reduce gun violence. But he says, "Being able to take care of patients is something that keeps me grounded and reminds me every day of what is important. Keeping patients in the center of the equation—that's a good principle to live by."

* * *

"Have I suffered burnout? Absolutely," he says. "But I have always had a very strong supportive network that allows me to deal with those low moments, when you're just completely exhausted physically and emotionally, and you don't have anything else to give.

"When I get to those points, I realize, OK, it's time to take a little bit of a break and spend a day or two doing nothing, or go on vacation. But I think I'm basically an optimistic person, and I always try to come to work with a cup-half-full perspective. I might be having the worst day personally, but I don't bring that to my work environment."

While not immune to burnout, Sakran thinks his near-death experience at 17 gives him a unique perspective.

"I was 17," he says. "Most 17-year-olds have no idea what they want to do for the rest of their lives. Most 17-year-olds don't realize that they are mortal. And most 17-year-olds don't appreciate the people that they have in their lives.

"When I got shot, it really opened my eyes, and the whole experience made me realize that I had been given a second chance," he continues. "To be able to provide other people with that same opportunity—that is what inspired my path into medicine. That moment when my father walked in as I was looking in the mirror feeling sorry for myself—when he told me I could feel sorry for myself or take the opportunity to try to make a difference for other people—that was a defining moment. It led me down this path, and inspired me to go into medicine, to become a trauma surgeon, and to work at the intersection of medicine, public health, and public policy."

The fragment of the bullet that came to rest in his left shoulder still sits on his dresser. He says, "I keep it there as a reminder of how lucky I am to be here, and how much I don't want to waste this second chance I have of life."

CHAPTER	Treating the
6	Whole Person

THE
GOOD
DOCTOR

LAURA MONSON KNEW what she knew, but she couldn't stop thinking about what she didn't know. It was 2012, and she was 34 years old, starting her first "real job" after years of training to become a pediatric plastic surgeon focusing on craniofacial problems. She had come to Texas Children's Hospital to operate on cleft lips and palates and other facial anomalies of young children. With many, if not most, of her patients, she would operate more than once, because staged approaches were demanded by their problems and the fact that they were growing.

She knew how to perform the operations, but as she interacted with patients and their parents over months and years, she found that she couldn't answer the questions that were really on their mind. Sure, she could tell them exactly what she planned to do, how much discomfort they could expect, and what the cosmetic result was likely to be. "But they wanted to know what their child's life was going to be like when they grew up," Laura recalls. "They wanted to know how having a cleft palate was going to affect them socially. How was it going to affect them academically? What

89

kind of jobs would they be able to get? Would they get married someday?

"I didn't have good answers for them," she said. "That was something I wanted to focus on."

Laura had been attracted to Texas Children's in part because the hospital's surgical leaders had a track record in collecting patient-reported outcome measures (PROMs) for pediatric cardiac surgery. They had data not just on whether patients survived their operations, but also on how they really fared. These kinds of outcomes can only be assessed by asking patients questions like, "Can you run and play with your friends?"

Laura knew such issues were especially important for her patient population. The surgical mortality was close to zero for the kind of patients she saw. Hardly anyone had craniofacial surgery to avoid death; they came for surgery because they hoped for a better quality of life. But there were hardly any data on the outcomes that mattered to her patients.

Laura wanted to start collecting PROMs data on her patients so she could start giving numbers rather than platitudes when she was asked what patients and families should expect. Collecting those data would take resources, and the return on that investment would not be realized for many years. After all, the outcomes that mattered were long-term, not measurable in a month or three months.

Laura's response to this concern was both pragmatic and audacious. "That's why we should start right away," she said.

Then she had an epiphany. Answering questions about what patients and families could expect was not going to be enough. Like any good surgeon, she wanted to change those outcomes for the better. She could improve and often completely correct the appearance of many children. Speech, singing, eating—these were more complex, but she had therapists who worked with her on those types of issues.

But having a normal social life? That meant trying to help her patients learn how much fun it is to act in a play or burst into song without feeling self-conscious. That meant helping them meet other children who had similar experiences, who after living in a cabin together, just might become their year-round friends and offer support beyond that provided by their family.

Laura realized that if she *really* wanted to help her patients she had to do more than perform surgery. So in 2014, she and her colleagues started Camp Keep Smiling for children ages 10 to 16 from the Texas Children's Cleft Lip and Palate Clinic. It's a camp like every other summer camp, with activities that include canoeing, fishing, archery, ropes courses, basketball, and arts and crafts. It also has chaperones (including Laura, her husband, and a host of volunteers from Texas Children's) on the prowl to make sure the kids don't have *too* much fun.

Unlike most camps, there is no charge, and there is an unusual purpose. As described on the website for the camp: "Children with cleft lip and palate tend to miss a lot of school for doctor and hospital visits. This can make it hard for them to make friends and fit in . . . Camp Keep Smiling provides a safe, fun environment for your child to engage in meaningful social interactions and gain self-confidence."

Laura Monson arrived at Texas Children's pretty sure she knew what she was doing with a scalpel in the operating room. A couple of years later she had realized that her therapeutic interventions should also include karaoke.

* * *

Laura grew up in Twin Lake, a western Michigan town of about 900 surrounded by farms. That rich farmland had attracted both sides of her family in the late 1800s. Laura, like almost all of her extended family—her parents, aunts, uncles, and cousins—went to Reeths-Puffer High School.

Her parents were high school sweethearts. Laura's father worked at a sprawling Brunswick factory that made bowling balls, pins, and pin-setting equipment until it closed in 2006. Laura's mother stayed at home with Laura and her older sister when they were young, and then went back to work as a librarian. Laura's sister lives with her family in northern Michigan and works as a medical assistant.

No one in Laura's family had previously gone to college, but she thinks she was exposed to just the right influences at home to prepare her for her work. She spent a lot of time with her mother in the library, which was next to her elementary school and across the street from her home. "I read a ton when I was a kid, partly because we moved a little bit outside of town, so it was hard to get to friends' houses," she recalls. "I spent most of the summer reading, sprawled across my bed or lying around outside. I was always getting in trouble for reading under the covers with a flashlight."

She traces her readiness to take on the mechanical challenges of surgery to time spent with her father. "In our family there was always a lot of emphasis on working with your hands," she recalls. "There was a lot to do around the house. My dad actually built our second house. There weren't any boys in the family, and I was always kind of a tomboy, so I helped him with that. There are photos of me putting the shingles on the roof when I was 13."

She says, "I loved school from the start, but I wasn't very good at actually going to it. I used to fake being sick a lot so I could stay home and read. I think I was a little bored."

In third grade, however, she had a teacher who was in his very first year. He started a program for talented and gifted children at her elementary school. "He was just phenomenal, and he showed me just how much impact a great teacher can have on students," she recalls. "The program was an after-school club for about 10 of us where we would build rockets and do various science experiments. It was 1986, the year the space shuttle *Challenger* exploded."

That teacher was the first person to tell Laura that she should definitely plan on going to college. With that goal clear in her mind, some of Laura's grown-up characteristics started to emerge. "I think my parents would say that I am stubborn," she says. "And I realize now that I began to feel competitive. I wasn't focused on beating other people, but if there was a spelling bee or a math contest, I really wanted to do my best. I was frustrated if I didn't."

* * *

If Laura had drive when she was a high school student, she wasn't sure where she was going. "I didn't see a clear path forward," she says. "There wasn't anybody around who made me think, 'That's how I see my life turning out.'

"I've always been very shy, and I didn't feel like I fit in that well in any group," she recalls. "I had some friends I'd go out with, but I didn't like going to dances and parties that much. I played softball and tennis, and I was in the rifle line, part of the color guard of the marching band. I did a little bit of lots of things.

"But I had to work, too. I started babysitting full time in the summers when I was 13, and once I had my driver's license I worked a couple of nights a week and on the weekends. They weren't great jobs. I worked at a sandwich shop and at one of those kiosks in the mall that makes popcorn—that kind of thing."

She did find time for the Science Olympiad, though, and took advanced placement classes in physics and calculus. She was near the top of her class.

Laura's mother was diagnosed with breast cancer when she was 13. In that same period, she lost relatives to other common malignancies—lung, colon, and ovarian cancers. The family illnesses made her think that she wanted to become a cancer researcher.

After high school, she went to Western Michigan University in Kalamazoo for a simple reason—she could afford it. Without a lot of financial aid, she would have had to go to a community college while working and living at home. But she really wanted to go away, so she applied for "probably a million" scholarships and got one from Western Michigan. She still needed part-time jobs—she worked in the library and tended bar on nights and weekends. And in fact, she had not really gone that far away— Kalamazoo and Twin Lake are only 99 miles apart. But she had left home to go to college, and she was determined to make the most of it.

* * *

A pattern began to emerge in which Laura would work hard and get what she was seeking only to discover it was less than she had hoped for. She would then open herself up to possibilities that were related but different, find something she loved, and plunge in.

So it was shortly after starting her freshman year that Laura found herself thinking, "What am I doing here?" She felt unprepared for college and was stressed by living away from her home and her friends and working extra jobs to make ends meet.

More important, she was disappointed with what she anticipated as the first big step toward her goal of becoming a researcher. She wanted to work on cures for terrible diseases, so she signed up to work in a neurology research laboratory. Her role there was preparing specimens and killing leeches. There was probably a connection between that work and a big important scientific question, but if there was, it was not apparent to Laura.

"I really, really didn't like it at all," she recalls.

But in her sophomore year, one friend who was training to become an emergency medical technician (EMT) and another who was going to pharmacy school said, "Why don't you come volunteer at this free health clinic? We could use help." Laura went and found the first college extracurricular activity that she really loved.

Volunteering at the clinic appealed partly because it aligned with the values she had been raised with. "My parents were always very proud of how I did in school, but it was never the most important thing," she says. "They put a lot of emphasis on being a good person, volunteering, and giving back. My mom was very involved in our church, and when someone was sick or in need, we would be making food and bringing it over."

Her work in the free clinic gave her a glimpse of the role that physicians could play in the lives of patients—and reinforced a positive impression from the past. "During my mom's illness, our primary care doctor was a real resource, someone who was really involved with our family," Laura recalls. "I realize now that, during college, I was trying to find something that really meant something—a job and a future that let me give back and do some good."

Laura had not been interested in medicine up until that point, because she didn't like many of the pre-med students she met. "They were so aggressive," she says. "We were in a lot of the same classes, and I just thought, this isn't what I want. I didn't see myself as being like them.

"But when I went to that free clinic and actually did work for people who really needed help, that was different. I was just doing patient intake, measuring the vital signs, and so on, but I really enjoyed it."

Halfway through her sophomore year, she decided that she wanted to be a doctor. College suddenly became much more enjoyable. She knew what she wanted to do, and she wasn't afraid to do the hard work necessary to get there. In her junior year, feeling the urge to broaden her horizons, she went to London and studied English history and literature, living in a flat with six other students. She came home to complete her last year at Western Michigan University and graduated summa cum laude in 2000.

* * *

Laura had decided that she wanted to do primary care in an inner-city population. She wanted to give the kind of care that had meant so much to her mother during her breast cancer treatment, and give it to the kind of population she had seen in the free clinic.

She interviewed at the three medical schools in Michigan. Again, for financial reasons, she couldn't look at schools all over the country. Wayne State University School of Medicine was the first to accept her, and because she was a Michigan resident, it was one of the least expensive. She immediately committed.

As had been true of college, the first year of medical school meant difficult adjustments. She was a country kid who had never lived outside western Michigan, and now she was living in one of the toughest urban areas in the country. "I was pretty sheltered," she says. "We had made very few trips to the eastern side of the state. I can remember going to a baseball game when I was young, and asking my parents why these people were on the street. It was the first time I had ever seen homeless people."

She describes living in Detroit as "eye-opening, and a little terrifying," but came to really enjoy it. And over the course of that first year, she learned how to do the type of studying that learning medicine required. "I struggled a bit, and definitely wondered if I had done the right thing," she says. "But I found a core group of friends who were very nerdy like I was. We studied in the basement of the library every night. Once I had that group, things got a lot better."

* * *

Just as Laura found her research experience in college a disappointment, she was disillusioned during her third year of medical school by her clinical experiences in primary care. "I did all my primary care first, and it just wasn't what I was looking for," she recalls. "It didn't feel like I was helping anybody. It didn't seem like there were solutions to most of the problems that people actu-ally came in with. So I was pretty worried.

"And then, at the very end of my third year, I did my surgery clerkship. I did trauma at Detroit Medical Center, and I loved it. I don't know why, but I just loved it."

Laura started thinking that she wanted to be a surgeon and was only mildly discouraged by well-intended advice that she should look for a less-demanding line of work. After all, she had received and ultimately ignored recommendations to avoid "the hard thing" before. When she was in high school, she told her guidance counselor she wanted to go to college and do research. The guidance counselor responded, "You can never go wrong with secretarial school." In college, her advisor said, "Medical school is a really long road. It's a hard life. It's a demanding life. Why don't you think about nursing?" Now in medical school, her friends and advisors were telling her that surgery was too hard and pediatrics was a better life.

Then during her fourth year, she watched a plastic surgeon do a breast reconstruction and thought, "That's just amazing." She had not even known what plastic surgery was. Someone told her, "If you really like children, and you really like plastic surgery, maybe you should check out pediatric plastic surgery at University of Michigan." She signed up for an elective there and decided this was exactly what she wanted to do.

"I think it was the feeling that you are really fixing something each and every time," she says. "But there is also a lot of counsel-ing and clinic time with the families. There was this one surgeon I worked with, Haskell Newman, who was in his late sixties or early seventies at the time. He kept trying to retire, but the fami-lies were begging him, 'No, please don't.'

"That was because so many patients needed surgeries that were staged over many years, and there were always patients and fami-lies that needed him to stay on for one more year. He had watched these kids grow up and been with their families through all of it, through finding out that their baby had a cleft palate, through all the trouble of middle school, and so on. There was something about the continuity that really just clicked with me."

Laura had discovered a field that blended what she liked from both primary care and surgery, and focused on a population of patients and families who were suffering deeply. It felt perfect.

"You should do this," Newman said to her. "You should definitely do this."

Laura was encouraged but worried that what she wanted was just out of reach. She knew that the odds of her getting into one of the premier surgery programs in the country (University of Michigan) from Wayne State were not good. (Wayne State's medical school is ranked slightly below the middle of the pack of the 141 US schools, while the University of Michigan's is near the top.) In fact, while she was on her elective at the University of Michigan, one of the leaders of the program said to her, "We're really glad to have you, and I hope you learn something while you are here. But we don't take students from Wayne State."

"Great," Laura thought to herself.

But the University of Michigan did in fact select her for its training program. Asked why, Laura says, "Because I worked my butt off. Hard work is hard work, and not everyone is willing to put in the time. They could tell how much I wanted it, and that I was never going to be a problem. I was always going to be super grateful that I had the opportunity. They had spent a month with me, and they knew what they would be getting. And they took me."

* * *

And so by July 2004, Laura—the first person in her family to go to college—had made her way from a small university an hour from home to a gritty state medical school to one of the top surgical training programs in the country (where another trainee was Mike Englesbe, from Chapter 2). She would work hard as a surgical resident from 2004 to 2011, including one year doing research. During that year, spanning 2008 and 2009, she operated on rat mandibles, making little devices that would go under their jaws and stretch them. "It was terrible," she says.

When it came time to apply for a fellowship in craniofacial surgery, she felt like the best fit for her was at University of Pittsburgh Medical Center (UPMC). It wasn't one of the top few programs in the country in terms of prestige, but during her interviews, those top few programs felt like old boys' clubs. She couldn't help but notice that she was usually the only female among about 30 applicants on interview day for surgical fellowships, and when she looked around for female professors in those departments, she wasn't finding any.

At UPMC, though, the feeling was different, more welcoming. The surgeon who would become her main mentor was gay, and there was a female faculty member already. The program seemed to be on the upswing, and there were close ties between the surgery departments at UPMC and the University of Michigan, with several faculty having worked at both. She signed on for one year at UPMC and immediately began looking for the "real" job that she would have after her fellowship.

* * *

Laura's resilience would be tested during that year at UPMC.

During the fall, she interviewed at several places that anticipated funding a position, but weren't able to make an offer when budgets were finalized in the spring. She interviewed at the University of Michigan, the institution at which she had trained, and accepted a position. She thought she was going home and was delighted.

But late in the spring, just a couple of months before her fellowship at UPMC was to end, she got a call on her cell phone while she was scrubbing for surgery. A nurse held her phone in front of her, and she could see the call was coming from a phone at the hospital at the University of Michigan. She ignored it, but then her phone rang again. It was the same number, and Laura decided she had better answer it. She was operating with her mentor, who said, "Yeah, absolutely, go take it."

She broke scrub and went out in the hallway to take the call. She learned that the funding for her position had been pulled back by the department of surgery. The person making the call had been her mentor at the University of Michigan for seven years, and he felt terrible about it. Laura just said, "OK, thanks for letting me know. I'll call you back when I know what I'm going to do."

And then she went back into the operating room and resumed the rest of her day.

"When I get news like that, I tend not to have a very large emotional reaction," she says. "It takes me a while to process things. I need to focus on getting my work done, and then I can let my mind race later."

Laura was in limbo, highly trained but without the job she would need in another eight weeks. She was also out of money. "You make very little as a fellow, and you're traveling everywhere to interview, paying out of pocket," she recalls. "I started to look at doing locum tenens work, anything. I started applying for privileges at hospitals in the Pittsburgh area. I was going to be doing wound care and staffing low-level ICUs and emergency departments. It wasn't the kind of work I had trained to do, but I needed to do something to keep the lights on.

"And then I heard that a position had opened up in Houston. My mentor in Pittsburgh said, 'You have to go interview.' And then he called Larry and said, 'You have to interview her.'"

* * *

"Larry" was Larry Hollier, MD, one of the country's leading plastic surgeons—someone with special focuses on craniofacial and cleft surgery as well as pediatric hand surgery. Larry is a meticulous surgeon, a highly respected expert on difficult problems like gunshot wounds of the face. He is high energy and intense. He has written hundreds of articles and book chapters, and given countless presentations. He has broad interests—and trouble saying no. As a result, he has been pulled into more and more activities outside and inside his institution, such as surgical training trips in Haiti, Africa, Central America, and Southeast Asia, and increasingly important roles leading care improvement at Texas Children's.

All of this became relevant in the spring of 2012 because it was very clear that Larry needed help. Laura's position at University of Michigan fell through at just the right time—just as Texas Children's started spreading the word that it was looking for someone to join Larry. Laura flew down to meet him in late May.

Laura and Larry were both decisive. Larry knew he wanted her, and Laura knew she wanted to come within a week. She signed her contract on June 23, 2012.

"It was just an amazing opportunity, and I couldn't believe my good luck," she said. "Texas Children's was the best-kept secret in the world of craniofacial surgery, and it was because they were so busy, they didn't have time to present their data at meetings very often." But now they really needed help. And Laura was ready.

* * *

When Laura joined the staff at Texas Children's Hospital, it was already nationally known as the largest pediatric hospital in the nation with top-rated programs in several areas. A Harvard Business School case study on its program for care of congenital heart disease describes how Texas Children's has organized terrific multidisciplinary teams to meet the full range of needs of children with these conditions. Part of that effort has been measuring PROMs and creating a culture of relentless work to improve them.

But that was cardiac surgery, not craniofacial surgery. Laura and Larry Hollier wanted to do for their patients what the surgeon-in-chief (a cardiac surgeon) had done for his. They wanted to measure the outcomes that mattered to their patients, and they wanted to organize great teams to improve those outcomes.

"The problem was that the outcomes that matter for our kids are different," Laura said. "For example, with adults with cardiac disease, the most important outcomes play out in 30 days—mortality, myocardial infarctions, strokes. But for our kids it could take 5 to 10 years to really get any handle on what's happening. And there are so few major clinical complications that you can measure, which makes it harder to demonstrate that you are improving.

"And the teams we need to care for patients must deal with so many issues," she continues. "We have to ask, do they have a good dentist? Are they getting the right speech therapy? Is the family as engaged as we want them to be?"

Laura looked at the number of patients with cleft lips and palates receiving care at Texas Children's—large by almost any other institution's standards, but small compared to the number of cardiac surgery patients. "You need large numbers to answer these questions," she says. "I thought to myself, my gosh, if they had just started collecting this information 10 years ago, we'd already have the answers to so many questions."

It was frustrating to her. That was when she made her comment during her job interviews about the long-term work of PROMs data collection, "We need to start this right away."

Laura made that comment to the surgeon (Charles Fraser) and nursing leader (Kathleen Carberry) who had led the congenital heart disease program development that was the focus of the

Harvard Business School case study, so she had a receptive audience. "I was trying to sell them on why they needed me," she said. "And I wanted them to know I was enthusiastic to get started right away."

* * *

It worked out. Laura moved to Houston and immediately had plenty of patients. At first, most were overflow from the many patients seeking care from Larry Hollier or the other established pediatric plastic and reconstructive surgeons, but now she has plenty of patients who come to Texas Children's specifically seeking her. The majority of her patients have cleft palate or lip, or other craniofacial anomalies. "Basically, I take care of anything that a child can be born with that makes them look different from their peers," she says.

By the time Laura arrived at Texas Children's, she knew that she was different from the big names in craniofacial surgery. They had established themselves by doing basic science research, studying how bones and other tissues developed, trying to get at the root causes of the diseases that affected their patients. Laura respected that work and is glad that she spent her time in the laboratory as a college student and surgical resident. Those experiences enable her to read papers and listen to presentations, and understand the questions that her laboratory-oriented colleagues are trying to answer. Such research may benefit patients who are not even born yet.

But Laura knows that what's right for her is taking care of the patients who are in front of her right now. Like her colleagues who are doing more traditional research, she has the long view, but it's a different kind of long view. She is looking way down the road for her patients and trying to figure out what will make their lives better a decade or so from now.

* * *

Here is how Laura got the idea of Camp Keep Smiling.

"One week in clinic, I was struck by two conversations I had with a couple of my teenaged patients," she said. "They were talking about some of the challenges they faced at school. They said they didn't have anybody to talk with about what it meant to have a cleft, and how they were treated.

"I thought back to some of the most challenging things I've been through in my life. I remembered how important it was at those times to have a friend who was either going through the same thing or who'd been through something similar. It helped just to be able to talk with them and feel like somebody understood what I was going through.

"Both of those patients had said they didn't know anybody else with a cleft. Now cleft is fairly common, affecting 1 in 700 kids. But if you're from a small town or from a small school, you may not know anybody else who has one.

"So I thought, 'Both of these girls feel like they are alone. But I know so many kids who are going through the same thing. What if I could just connect them?' So that was how the idea of the camp came to be."

* * *

Part of Laura's vision for the camp was that finances would not be a barrier for children or their families, so the first step was raising funds. Larry Hollier stepped right in and found the resources for his young protégé to get the project off the ground. It continues to get funded through philanthropy for at least one session a year, sometimes two. For a few years, Laura had a grant from the state to study interventions that might improve quality of life in these patients. Finding the funds is a perpetual part of the adventure, as are the three-day sessions themselves.

The camp is in Burton, Texas—about 90 miles from Texas Children's Houston location. About 50 or 60 children come every year. The staff are all volunteers from Texas Children's. There are nurses from the clinic, hospital floors, and operating rooms. There are doctors, surgical technicians, physician assistants, schedulers, and receptionists. The hospital allows employees to use a few days a year for volunteer work, so that institutional policy has helped make the camp viable.

Laura's physician assistant, Michelle Roy, coordinates everything—and there is a lot to coordinate—contracts for the buses that transport the children to and from the hospital and the camp, insurance forms, and other endless paperwork. The detail work is offset for Michelle by the fun of the theme planning.

"This year we are having a rodeo theme, but other years we've done a Halloween camp with a haunted trail and trick-or-treating," Laura says. The kids get a swag bag full of stuff that fits with the theme. We have a dance party on Saturday night that is probably overdecorated, but we really enjoy it. The staff is into it, too."

Read the blog posts by campers, and you can't miss the evidence that Laura's sense of what her patients needed was correct. There is plenty of text about camp features, like "free ice cream," and descriptions of how it felt to use a zip line for the first time. But buried among these paragraphs are sentences like, "Soon after arriving at camp, I met all of the people in my cabin and made tons of friends. It was cool to attend camp with other kids who have cleft lip and palate. I knew that every other camper (and some counselors) had similar experiences as me."

* * *

As for Laura herself, the outcomes that matter are good and getting better. Laura recently was asked to become chief quality and safety officer for the department of surgery. That has meant cutting her clinical time back to 50 percent and concentrating her care on patients with cleft lip and palate.

Her family life outside work is as intense as life inside Texas Children's. She has a daughter born in 2014 and a son born in the spring of 2019. When he isn't helping out at Camp Keep Smiling, her husband is a researcher, studying alternative energy sources. "We have a crazy work-life balance, and somehow we make it all work," she says.

* * *

I met Laura for the first time in 2015, not long after she had gotten the camp off the ground. I asked if she had to worry about the kids sneaking off in the woods and doing what teenagers do at other camps. She laughed and said, "Not so far. But many of these children have only been kissed by their parents. In a way, what you are talking about would be a good problem to have."

Three years later, she emailed me to tell me that she now had the problem. "I mean, we've got 16-year-olds, and they have been coming back year after year, and staying in touch in between," she says. "We make sure that the oldest boys' and the oldest girls' cabins are very far away from each other. The counselors are always sleeping by the door.

"We have a lot of ingenious ways of making sure that nobody leaves their cabins at night. Part of the decorations in their cabins include some kind of noisemaker that's attached to the door, so we know if the door gets opened.

"We've never had any real issues. Our kids are very respectful. Everyone signs a code of conduct that they know they have to follow.

"But we do have three couples now from the camp. They are dating. Their families have met. They've been to prom together and to homecoming.

"It's really very sweet."

* * *

How many surgeons bring up prom dates when they talk about their patients' outcomes? It couldn't have happened if Texas Children's had not already been interested in measuring PROMs, and if they hadn't hired a young surgeon who really wanted to take care of her patients. She not only wanted to capture data on the measures that mattered to her patients—she wanted to change them for the better, even before the data started coming in.

She understood that there was a long game that mattered to her patients, and she was determined to be a player in it.

Delivering Care to Those in the Greatest Need

IN JANUARY 2016 Lara Johnson, took the stage in a school auditorium in East Dallas, Texas, not far from where she had graduated as valedictorian at Woodrow Wilson High School 23 years before. It was an event to thank high school teachers from around the region, and the crowd in the auditorium was probably expecting a pep talk of sorts—a tribute to Lara's favorite teacher explaining how she had helped launch her on a path to becoming a primary care physician at nearby Parkland Health and Hospital System.

During her nine-minute talk (captured on video and posted at https://vimeo.com/253774401), the audience laughed as Lara admitted that she was nervous. It was her first time speaking to a large group since that valedictory speech. But then the audience fell silent as Lara said, "I am thrilled that I am here sharing my story with you, and not at a 12 Step Program, because things could have gone really differently.

"Growing up the child of a drug-addicted mother and an alcoholic father presents some unique challenges," Lara continued. "You learn to read the emotional temperature of a room, and you learn how to defuse things. You learn how to try to put out fires rather than adding fuel to them. Passivity becomes a survival skill, and you spend a lot of your life as a quiet spectator rather than an active participant.

"When the adults around you can barely take care of themselves, you learn early on that you have to take care of yourself. You set your own alarm clock in the morning, you make your own breakfast, you pack your lunch, you do your own laundry, and a lot of days, you have to wake up an adult to take you to school.

"The one thing you learn to rely on is that you can't rely on anything. The TV that you watched last night might be in the pawnshop today. The toilet might not flush because the water bill went unpaid—again. Your aunt might be sleeping on the sofa, sometimes alone, other times with a boyfriend. Your mom might not come home at night, and you find yourself actually hoping that she is in jail, where at least you know she is safe and not on the street.

"You begin to notice the cycles of the addict. There is the short-lived cycle—the longing, the planning, the doing whatever needs to be done to obtain the money, obtain the drugs or alcohol. Sometimes this meant popping hubcaps off cars at stoplights and other times shoplifting tools from Home Depot. Then there is the release, the relief from the pain, which is always too brief, which is followed quickly by the return of the misery and the ugliness that is left behind when the high fades.

"There is a bigger cycle that you begin to notice, too. Sobriety, followed by employment sometimes, and the blossoming of hope. Occasionally, we would move into our own place. Saving money, being picked up at school on time, and waking up in the morning to the sound of coffee percolating and the local news.

"But this, too, would always crash down, usually in a matter of months. The savings spent, the apartment gone, the job lost, moving back in with the grandparents who were always loving but nevertheless disappointed to see us return.

"These cycles taught me what I did not want for my own life. I did not want to suffer the way I watched my mother suffer when she could not get heroin—or worse, when she tried to kick methadone."

At this point, Lara paused, then she apologized, her voice cracking. She explained that her mother had recently died, and her story was difficult to tell. She then continued, describing the many other aspects of her childhood that she knew she wanted to avoid. "That's how I thought of my future—in negatives," she said. "They were healthy negatives, but they were negatives."

But then she described how everything changed during her senior year at Woodrow Wilson. A teacher named Patricia Faherty had grasped both Lara's academic potential and her difficult situation at home. Faherty asked her why she hadn't applied to college, what she hoped to become. "She helped me to fill in the positive," Lara continued. "She helped me flesh out my future."

The deadlines for applying to college had passed, but Faherty told Lara that didn't matter and that she should try to go. But Lara's responsibilities at home had only grown during her senior year of high school. Her father had been diagnosed with AIDS (and this was just before the 1994 development of highly active antiretroviral therapy, the combinations of drugs that made HIV a controllable condition). Lara was living with him, preparing his meals, managing his medications.

"He was getting weaker by the week," Lara said. "And my mom had just started using crack cocaine. She would often show up at Tom Thumb where I worked as a cashier and ask to borrow 20 bucks.

"How could I think about leaving?" she wondered. Faherty told her that she had to go and took steps to change her life. She signed Lara up for Advanced Placement tests without her knowledge—just telling her when to show up. Faherty paid the fees for the tests, and Lara said, "She basically put a pencil in my hand, and said go.

"And then she did something even more remarkable," Lara continued. "One spring afternoon, she invited me to her East Dallas home. . . . There on her living room sofa, she and her husband offered to pay for my college education. I just had to meet three conditions.

"One, maintain a C or better average . . .

"Two, move at least an hour away from Dallas, so I would be out of hitchhiking range for my mom.

"And three, do the same for someone else someday."

Lara described how she took the Fahertys up on their offer. She did her best to arrange things for her father, but also shifted her attention to the future. She got into a college that was nearby, but not too nearby. She began to communicate with her future roommate. When the fall came, she left for college.

In her talk, Lara described how eventually she went to the University of Texas Southwestern Medical School. As a child, she had visited UT Southwestern's Parkland Memorial Hospital countless times with her mother, as she received antibiotics and other care, including brain surgery for complications of her addiction.

"I used to marvel at the doctor and nurses, silently praying that they would not only cure my mother, but also treat her kindly," Lara said. "For the past eight years, I have been working for Parkland, serving the pediatric and adult homeless population. We take a big medical unit out to homeless shelters, domestic violence shelters, drug rehab facilities, and juvenile detention centers.

"Now I have the honor of caring for people who have the same types of struggles that my family faced," she said. "I often wonder what would my life look like, where I would be if I hadn't gone to Woodrow, enrolled in AP English, and met Patricia Faherty. She taught me to believe in myself. There is no question—teachers change lives every day. Thank you for what you do."

*   *   *

A few months after giving that talk at her high school and describing how she had gone so many times with her mother to Parkland Memorial Hospital, Lara took on a new role. After a decade as a primary care physician at Parkland Health, Lara Johnson became the medical director for Parkland's HOMES program (Homeless Outreach Medical Services). It was a big step for her; Parkland is *the* safety net hospital for Dallas, the place that never turns anyone away because of lack of insurance. That is why Lara's mother had gone there.

Lara is the key clinical leader for two clinics that are part of homeless shelters in downtown Dallas. The program also has five mobile medical units that go around to about 25 different sites in Dallas County—not only homeless shelters, but also domestic violence shelters, juvenile detention facilities, a day care center for homeless children, family shelters, and drug rehabilitation shelters.

She and her colleagues have an atypical patient population and tight resource constraints, but they basically do what clinicians do everywhere—whatever they can to help their patients be as healthy as possible. They provide primary care preventive services, cancer screenings, and vaccines, as well as urgent care. And like clinicians everywhere, they frequently feel frustrated by the systems around them and experience symptoms of "burnout"—feeling overwhelmed, ineffective, and detached from their work. Yes, the work is noble, but it doesn't always feel that way.

Lara herself is not immune to burnout symptoms, and she isn't so sure how she feels about managing about 50 colleagues, compared to rolling up her sleeves and delivering primary care to one patient at a time. But she doesn't have trouble feeling genuine empathy for the patients she meets in the shelters where she and her team go. After all, she and her family have walked in their shoes.

Today, her life is a happy chaos filled with what so many others seek—a good job, a good marriage to a respected professional, two young children, and a nice house in one of the country's great cities. But Lara never forgets the difference between happy chaos and unhappy chaos. She grew up with the latter, which is why her current work, even when overwhelming or frustrating, never feels unimportant.

* * *

Until recently, Lara didn't discuss her past very often, but in 2014 she was sitting around a swimming pool with another mother, keeping their eyes on their children. Conversation turned to their family backgrounds, and what came out stunned Lara's friend. She was a journalist and said Lara's story was a great one, and that it should be told. The result was "How a Teacher Changed This Dallas Doctor's Life," by Jamie Thompson, published in *D Magazine* in October 2015. It was a valuable source for parts of this chapter.

The story that emerges from that article and my additional interviews with Lara is beyond complex. Her mother was a heroin addict who worked as a waitress and night-shift office cleaner. Her father was an alcoholic who also was a heroin user for a while and ran a pool cleaning company with his brother. Besides her parents' addictions and related medical issues, there were other relatives with problems of their own.

The family tree is hard to draw. Both parents had brief first marriages that produced a half-brother and half-sister for Lara. Lara's parents had younger siblings who married each other. A reasonable reaction is amazement that someone as strong and stable as Lara somehow emerged from this chaos. But to Lara, they are all just her family. She doesn't try to distance herself from them and their troubles; she talks about them with love and a wry pride.

Both of Lara Johnson's parents grew up in Dallas, and like she did, both went to Woodrow Wilson High School. There were glimpses of glory in the family tree—an uncle who was a track star, and a grandfather who had played bass in the Tommy Dorsey Orchestra. There were also problems with alcohol. Both of her father's parents had been alcoholics, but her father's mother was in Alcoholics Anonymous (AA) and sober for more than three decades.

When Lara talks about her father, she doesn't just describe his addictions. She also brings up good advice he gave her and funny things he said and did. "My dad was a major character," she says. "He liked to play pranks on people, but not in a mean-spirited way. I think he enjoyed seeing how they would react. I feel like he was always running his own little psychology experiments."

After Lara's father graduated from high school in 1965, he got married, had a child, and went to Vietnam. Lara has a photo of him from those years hanging in a hallway in her home. In the photo, he is smiling, looking handsome and fit in his Air Force uniform, but Lara is pretty sure that he came home from Vietnam with a drug problem.

"It's funny—no, not funny, but interesting—to think about the kind of conversations that I would have as an adult that of course you don't have with your parent when you're a teenager," she says. "So there are a lot of things that I don't know, and that I'll never know."

Lara's father's forebears had come to Dallas from Sicily, New Orleans, and Chicago, drawn by the availability of work. His parents ran a 24-hour bowling alley called the Cotton Bowling Palace. One of the regulars in the years before 1963 was Jack

Ruby—the nightclub owner who shot Lee Harvey Oswald after the assassination of President John Kennedy. Ruby used to drop by the Cotton Bowling Palace after his own clubs shut for the night at 2 a.m., sit with Lara's grandfather, smoke cigarettes, and drink coffee.

Lara's mother was four years behind Lara's father at Woodrow Wilson High School, and later told Lara that she began having problems with opioids when she was 19. "Both of my parents had terrible teeth," Lara says. "My dad had dentures before he was 20, in part because a lot of them got knocked out in a fist fight. My mom just had teeth problems, and she needed major dental work. That's when she initially got hooked on pain meds, and it escalated through the years. That's why my sister and I are both crazy fanatics about oral hygiene."

When Lara looks further back in her mother's life story, she thinks her mother had mental health struggles from an early age—anorexia and probably more. "My grandmother told me that when my mom was a really young child, like five or seven years old, a pediatrician asked my grandparents to take her to a psychiatrist," Lara says. "This was the 1950s, and my grandfather just said, 'No way. My kid is not going to a nut doctor.'" So one of the things that has been painful for Lara is contemplating how her mother's life could have been better or different if she had gotten the treatment that she needed when she was young.

Lara's mother was briefly married shortly after she graduated from high school, and she had Lara's half-sister when she was 19 years old. A few years later, that marriage had ended, and she married Lara's father, who was now back from Vietnam. They got married on New Year's Eve of 1972, and Lara was born New Year's Eve of 1974. "My dad loved parties and threw a party every year on my birthday until he died," Lara says. "My mom hated parties, so when she went into labor the day I was born, my dad didn't believe her. He thought she was just trying to get out of the party, so he didn't go with her to the hospital. He came eventually, but it meant he had to cancel his New Year's Eve party."

* * *

Lara's parents' marriage only lasted a few years. They both were addicted to heroin, and problems reached a crisis point when Lara was two. "On the night that my mom left my dad, there was some domestic violence, and he actually pulled a gun and fired some shots," Lara says. "He was too drunk to hit his mark, thankfully, but my mom did a very courageous thing and left. My sister and I spent the night in an emergency shelter."

Lara, her mother, and her sister eventually moved into the home of her mother's parents. "They were gracious enough to house us on and off throughout my life," Lara says. "They were my safety net, and my sister's safety net."

But it was still a wild environment, because of the drug addictions of Lara's mother and her aunt—Lara's mother's younger sister—who came to live with them after being released from federal prison, where she had served a sentence of several years.

"She was actually a hilarious person," Lara recalls. "She was an artist. She and my mom would go out and steal and do drugs, and then they'd come back at night, and my mom would make up lies about what they had been doing. But my aunt would be honest with my sister and me in a way that we found very refreshing."

That aunt had an unexpected pregnancy when Lara was around 12, and Lara was thrust into the role of helping to raise the baby boy because her mother and aunt were simply unable. "I can remember getting really angry when he'd wake up in the morning and need things," Lara recalls. "But my mother and aunt would be too altered to address his needs. So I would get up with him and take care of him.

"I am not someone who is quick to anger, but when they would yell at him, that would just push me over the edge," she says. "And

I would walk him to McDonald's, just to get out. I was 13, and he was a year or so old. People would think he was my kid, and I would get furious. I would say, 'He's my cousin. I'm not a teen mom.'"

* * *

Well before this point, Lara had her introduction to healthcare—and to Parkland Hospital at its best. When Lara was in fourth grade, her mother started to have neurological symptoms. She turned out to have a mass in her brain that was caused by a fungal infection—almost surely resulting from injecting heroin with nonsterile needles.

Lara had been to the hospital and various clinics with her mother countless times in the past, often as she sought opioids as treatments for headaches or other symptoms. Her mother frequently complained that she was not being treated with respect because she had a history of drug-seeking behavior.

But this time, the neurosurgery fellow was a young man named Dr. Bruce Mickey, and Lara has never forgotten how he interacted with her mother. "He treated my mom the way he treated all of his patients," Lara says. "He treated her like a queen. He was respectful. He didn't seem judgmental. He didn't blame her for this infection in her brain, which was probably caused by her behaviors.

"It was a revelation for me. She was in the hospital for six weeks after her surgery getting amphotericin (an antifungal medication), and I was up there almost every day after school, camped out at Parkland Hospital as a nine-year-old."

Dr. Mickey remains on staff at Parkland Hospital today and is vice chair of the Department of Neurological Surgery at UT Southwestern Medical Center. Lara is now his colleague. She has told him of this early memory and how it may have helped plant an early seed in her thinking about becoming a physician.

In any case, when she was in seventh grade, she wrote an essay in response to an assignment to project her future. She wrote that she would be a pediatrician living in New England with two adopted children. When Lara looks back on that essay today, she says that being a pediatrician is not that different from doing what she does in family practice.

She ended up staying in Dallas, though, and having her own biological children. "My sister has no kids," she says. "Pretty much no one in my family in my generation has kids except for me. Everyone else was too traumatized by the experience, I think."

* * *

Lara and her mother and sister periodically moved out of Lara's grandparents' home and tried to make a go of it on their own. By the time Lara was in eighth grade, she had been to 11 different elementary schools.

At 13, she made a decision that enabled her to have something approaching a normal adolescence. Her father had long since given up heroin, and although he had serious alcohol problems, he had decided to quit drinking and join AA. He had been able to buy a small house in East Dallas with his VA benefits. Lara decided that living with her father was going to be more stable and moved in with him. She was able to stay in the same school from that point until she graduated.

As difficult as things with her father were from time to time, Lara remembers plenty of loving, wonderful moments. "One thing about my dad—he taught me to be independent!" she says. "When I was just 12, he would tell me to take the truck and pick up something from the store. I'd say, 'Dad, I don't have a license.' And he'd say, 'You can do it. It's not far. There's just one stop sign. Just go slow. You'll be fine.'"

She made those short drives, and things did work out just fine.

Meanwhile, Lara figured out that she liked school—a lot. "It was a place I could go that was structured and calm," she says. "I could focus on something that wasn't my family. I could get all this adult attention, and if I did well, it felt pretty good."

Her senior year yearbook photo lists activities including cross country, swim team, art club, National Honor Society, student council, cheerleading, choir, and school musicals. "I was doing everything," she recalls. "And I was working, too. My senior year, I worked in a retirement home as waitstaff. A couple of my friends were there, too, and it was a blast. And then in the spring, I was a cashier at a grocery store. So I was kind of busy."

During these high school years, her father would often keep her company while she did her homework at the kitchen table. But during her senior year, he started to get sick and was in and out of the hospital. "He was struggling with the fact that he couldn't do all the things he wanted to do," she says. "He said to me, 'You need to be comfortable with more quiet in your life. You go all the time, and you're not always going to be able to do that.'"

But Lara was getting a different type of advice from her English teacher, Patricia Faherty. Early each fall, Faherty had her students write an autobiographical essay. Lara's began with her mother saying, "I am done. I will never do heroin again." And then Lara wrote that, even though she had heard those words dozens of times before, she always took them as gospel.

That essay showed Faherty that Lara could not only write, but also had been through so much in life already and remained resilient. Faherty took special interest in Lara, and as the year went on, noticed that Lara did not ask her for a letter of recommendation for college, even though she was one of the school's top students. Faherty asked the other teachers if they had written recommendations for her. None had. Faherty realized that Lara was not applying to college at all.

That was when they had the conversations that Lara described in her 2016 talk. Lara just didn't see how she could go away and leave her father when he was so sick, or cut herself off from her mother when she was still using heroin. Besides, she had no money to pay for school. And in any case, the key deadlines had passed.

That is when Faherty and her husband made their offer to pay for her education. In the following weeks, she helped Lara complete applications and round up her recommendations. Lara started to talk about whether she might become a physical therapist. Faherty said she should aim higher—try to become a doctor.

"At the time, when I was 18 years old, the money seemed like the biggest gift," Lara says. "The money, of course, made it possible and was a phenomenal thing to have happened. But now that I have a lot more years under my belt, I realize that it was so much more than that. It was having someone see the potential in you and help you see it in yourself."

When graduation came around, Lara was valedictorian, finishing ahead of one student who headed to Princeton and another who went to Stanford. Lara had gotten into Trinity University, a private liberal arts college in San Antonio. Her classmates voted her "Most Likely to Succeed."

* * *

Despite Faherty's amazing act of generosity, Lara's transition to her new life was far from smooth. In March of Lara's senior year, her father gave her a letter from his physician at the VA with news that was too painful to convey directly himself. He was HIV positive and now had AIDS. He had been trying to delay delivering this news until after her graduation, but he was becoming increasingly ill, and he was worried that he wasn't going to survive that long. "He passed away on June 20, 1993," Lara recalls. "It was Father's Day."

A couple of months later, Lara left for San Antonio. She and her high school boyfriend were both going to school in San Antonio, and Lara spent a lot of time with her boyfriend's family before school started. The night before she left for college, her mother showed up at her boyfriend's house, where Lara was having dinner with his parents. It wasn't clear how she got there—she didn't have a car. But what was clear was what she wanted—money. "It was embarrassing, and I was angry," Lara recalls. "I was thinking, this is the send-off that I get?"

She arrived at school the next day. "I felt like I was the only kid who didn't have a parent there helping them set up their room," she says.

* * *

Lara got through her first year at Trinity and came home to Dallas for the summer. She had not been happy at school. She had started as pre-med, but really didn't like it. "Everyone was super-intense, super-competitive," she says. "I just felt that these were not my people. It did not feel good." So she switched to anthropology, and the idea of becoming a doctor faded away.

She also wasn't happy with her relationship with her high school boyfriend—one more reason that she was not excited about going back to San Antonio in the fall. She was working in a bank doing customer service in August 1994, when she met a young man who had just graduated from medical school. He had come to the bank because his mother had multiple sclerosis and he was organizing her financial affairs. He was also cleaning out her house, and he had a week or so before he himself was going to move to Memphis where he would start his internship in a family practice program. They hit it off, and she started spending her off hours helping him pack up the house. Ten days later, Lara decided to go to Memphis with him.

Lara transferred to the University of Memphis and started working at another bank in her new city—but she liked what she was seeing about medicine. "When I met the other interns and residents that Joe was training with, I thought, 'Oh, I like these people. They don't seem crazy and cutthroat,'" she recalls. So she started taking pre-med courses at the University of Memphis. She married Joe, the family practice resident, when she was 21 and then moved back to Dallas when he got a job there after his training. She completed her college education in December 1997 at the University of Texas at Arlington. She was almost 23 years old and graduated summa cum laude. She was accepted for medical school at UT Southwestern.

* * *

Lara had survived a tumultuous childhood, gone to three different colleges, and now was accepted at one of the top medical schools in the country, where she would walk the halls with Nobel Prize winners like cholesterol researchers Michael Brown and Joseph Goldstein.

"Who would have thought?" she says, with a laugh. "It's funny because when I think of my mom, I have to say she was brilliant. The way her brain worked was just fascinating to me. She was so quick. She would read voraciously—finish a 300-page book in two or three days. She always did crossword puzzles, and she was a math wizard.

"We used to have this game figuring out what we could buy with the money we had when we went to the grocery store. It was a necessity because we didn't have a lot of money. We never had a credit card or a checking account. We were completely cash-based. But she made it into a game, and she'd like to see who could get the closest to the actual total. In Texas, certain food items aren't taxed, and certain ones are—so calculating the tax made it complicated. But it was fun, and she was so quick.

"She had a really funny sense of humor," Lara adds. "When she wasn't horrible, she was wonderful."

* * *

Medical school was an eye-opening experience for Lara. She had not realized it, but schoolwork had come all too easily for her in the past, and she hadn't had to work that hard to get almost straight As throughout high school and college. Now she was working constantly and getting mostly As, but also a few Bs despite her best efforts. "It was a real adjustment, and the first time I *really* had to study," she says. "One friend and I became study partners, and if not for her, I don't know how I would have done. She was so very disciplined and organized. We are still really good friends. But it was hard."

When her clinical training began in her third year, though, she was thrilled. "It was exhausting, but so much fun," she says. "I had started medical school thinking I wanted to do family medicine, but then I really loved my surgery rotation. I actually applied to both surgery and family medicine, and ultimately decided that surgery would be fun for 5 or 10 years, but I didn't see doing it for 30 years.

"I thought family medicine would be something I would always find interesting. I mean, I love hearing people's stories. As goofy as that sounds, I wanted that continuity and the ongoing relationships with patients, which you don't have in some of the other specialties."

After medical school, she did her family practice residency in Fort Worth, in the John Peter Smith Family Practice Residency. It was one of the premier family medicine programs in the country, in part because there were no "competing" programs in internal medicine or emergency medicine. The family medicine residents like Lara did everything. "I did tons of colonoscopies, and delivered 200 babies when I was there," she recalls. "It was drinking from the fire hydrant. Some of the people I trained with are in rural settings and basically working like general surgeons—doing appendectomies, gallbladders, and C-sections. They are like *real* doctors. You definitely got confidence that you could do a lot of things."

Meanwhile, at the end of her second year of medical school, her marriage to Joe had come to an amicable end. They remain good friends today, and he was Lara's mother's primary care physician up until the time of her death. He also was the physician for Lara's grandmother and aunt.

During her fourth year of medical school, she met David Gerber, an internal medicine resident at UT Southwestern. Lara's best friend at medical school, Elizabeth Dodge, had gone to college at Yale with David, and they met through that connection. They started dating in October 2001. After his residency, he went to Johns Hopkins for a fellowship in medical oncology. They were engaged at that point, and Lara went to Baltimore to be with him when she finished her own training. They married in May 2005.

* * *

Lara and David did not know where they would end up, and Lara took advantage of the uncertainty by getting some new experiences while David was finishing his Hopkins fellowship. "I didn't want to start a practice or look for a job that I thought I would be leaving after a year or two, and I always feel like I need more training," she says. "So I did a one-year faculty development and medical editing fellowship at Georgetown. And the clinical portion of my fellowship was at a homeless healthcare center in Washington, DC. I didn't pick the fellowship because of the homeless care focus, but it turned out to be very important for me."

After that one-year fellowship, she spent a year as a staff physician at the Baltimore VA Medical Center. That role felt comfortable to her, too. "My dad went to the VA in Dallas, and my mom went to Parkland," she says. "I knew I wanted to work with underserved populations like the ones I saw there. It's just always been where my heart is."

In 2007, David and Lara returned to UT Southwestern and Parkland Hospital—and have stayed. He specializes in lung cancer. Lara became a staff physician in the homeless outreach program. She has also started working at the Good Shepherd Hospice and at Parkland's transgender clinic. She was appointed medical director for the homeless outreach program in June 2018. They have two children, 10 and 12 years old.

* * *

Lara worked at the Good Shepherd Hospice for three years, but quit in May 2015, shortly before her mother died. "It was too close to home," she recalls. But thoughts about her parents linger in the professional work that she continues.

Asked how her parents' medical care had influenced her choices, she says, "I think part of it is still wanting to heal my parents. They are both dead, of course, but I see a lot of people who face the same kinds of struggles that my parents faced. I see a lot of substance abuse, a lot of mental health issues, a lot of tough situations.

"It is simplistic to say that I always want to root for the underdog, but that's kind of what it feels like."

She describes seeing a patient in the transgender clinic who did not reveal his heroin use during his first clinic visit, but told a nurse about it during his return appointment. The nurse came and got Lara out of her room, and asked her to talk to the patient.

Lara went in and sat on the floor, because that was the easiest way to make reliable eye contact with him. "I told him that I was glad that he trusted us with that information, and that our goal was to try to help him," she recalls. "I said that it was human instinct to try to alleviate suffering, and any of us—if we are suffering, we are going to use whatever we have around us to relieve it. Some people use alcohol because it works. Some people use drugs because they work."

The patient revealed that he had been diagnosed with a psychotic disorder and wasn't taking any prescribed medications for it. But, he said, when he took heroin, the voices in his head stopped.

"I get it," Lara says. "I've never done heroin, and I'm terrified of it. But if you find something that makes you feel somewhat normal for some amount of time—well, I'm not going to judge someone for that. I'm going to try to help them get to a better place, but I'm not going to look at it like a moral failure."

* * *

Before Lara's mother died, she would frequently visit Lara and her family. When Lara's daughter Allie was only three, Lara noticed that she made a face when she heard that Grandmother Kathy was coming over. When Lara asked why, Allie said, "You get really sad when she is here."

Knowing that risk of addiction is at least partially genetic, Lara is extremely cautious about alcohol. "I am of course scared about the potential of addiction in me, and I didn't drink at all during college—zero, none," she says. "Now, I may have a drink or two a week, but not on the same day. I want to be a model for good responsible behavior for the kids. If we go out and I am going to have a glass of wine, I make a point of mentioning that Dad is going to drive home tonight. This is a decision that we're making."

Lara is new to her role as medical director, and there are frustrations in managing dozens of colleagues. "People at work will say, 'Just go home and have a drink. A glass of wine a day will fix that,'" she says. "I just laugh, and think, 'Yeah, whatever.'

"I know I need to be a better leader," she says. "I have to get better at figuring out how to make people tick and fight the tendency to just want to do things myself. And now I only get to see patients myself two half-days a week. When I'm there, I'm thinking, this is what I'm meant to be doing. That is what feels rewarding to me."

Lara says she understands the symptoms of burnout and has felt them herself from time to time. "But the funny thing to me is that I don't remember feeling that way when I was doing only clinical care," she says. "A big reason is that I love my coworkers. I look forward to being on that mobile unit, interacting with the driver, who is also our financial front desk person when we're on a mobile clinic. I have relationships with all of them. They're so important to our team. They're the first people that our patients see, and some of them have incredible stories. The nurses are just phenomenal—so strong.

"Many of them have endured troublesome pasts as well, whether it's family members with addiction or losing siblings to suicide. So even on the days I am tired and feeling the bed was the better option, the thought of seeing the people that I work with, and then seeing the patients as well is always enough to get me out of bed."

* * *

Lara quotes one of her paternal grandmother's favorite sayings: The key to a happy life is a grateful heart. "It sounds goofy," she says. "But I believe that. I think that every day, if we can think about the things that we're grateful for, it does change your outlook.

"I try every day to be grateful for my family, my children, their health, the stability that my husband and I have been able to provide for them. I think having lived through a time when things didn't feel certain, and when bad things could happen and did happen routinely and unexpectedly, helped me really appreciate the predictability and the calm that comes with steady employment and knowing where you're going to be every day, and having clean clothes, and having reliable transportation, and having mental health and physical health."

She hasn't forgotten what she owes to Patricia Faherty and her husband. "Pay it forward—I know I have to do that," she says. "Help someone else out when you're in the position to be able to do that."

She is quick to say that she and her husband have not sent anyone to college—yet. But she mentions someone she knows from the homeless outreach program, whose daughter is thinking about medical school. Lara has her eye on her.

Never Giving Up

BABACAR CISSE, MD, PHD, a 45-year-old neurosurgeon at Weill Cornell Medicine, is not technically a Dreamer—one of immigrants who are the focus of the Development, Relief, and Education for Alien Minors (DREAM) Act. The DREAMER legislation was introduced in 2001, outlining a multistep process that would grant conditional residency and, upon meeting other qualifications, permanent residency for undocumented aliens who were younger than 18 years of age upon initial entry to the United States.

Cisse was already 24 years old when he got off a plane from Senegal at JFK Airport in 1998. He had graduated from high school in 1993 in Dakar, the capital of Senegal, but had no other degrees. In his pockets, he had just $26, a student visa, and a piece of paper with the address of a cousin. At that point, he did not know that his visa would soon lapse because he could not afford tuition. He almost immediately learned from a taxi driver that the street on that address in the Bronx did not exist. The driver knew a street with a similar name, but $26 was not going to get him even close to that address.

Cisse had no bank account, no credit card, and no other contacts aside from a cousin whom he barely knew and could not reach. But the taxi driver, an immigrant himself, took pity on him and drove him around the Bronx in search of the right address. They couldn't find it, so the taxi driver took him home to his tiny apartment, offered him dinner (he ordered from a Chinese restaurant), and let him sleep on the couch. In the morning, they started again and found the cousin.

Screenplays are written about days like Cisse's first 24 hours in America. But that day was neither the first nor the last time that Babacar Cisse ran into problems that might have dashed his hopes.

Two months later, he was an undocumented immigrant working as a busboy in a Midtown restaurant. But during his breaks, when other busboys might relax outside and smoke, he went to the New York Public Library and scoured college catalogs, searching for a place where he could get a college education. He was eager to start down the road to becoming a legal citizen and finding a job where he could pursue what had been the core value of his family for generations—doing good for others.

Because of his resilience, hard work, and a series of mentors who saw his potential and loved his warm personality, he got into and graduated from Bard College and earned MD and PhD degrees at Columbia University. He then trained in one of the top neurosurgery programs in the world, and joined the staff at Weill Cornell Medical College and New York Presbyterian Hospital. Today, he cares for patients with brain tumors and other neurosurgical conditions, and runs a large grant-funded laboratory performing research.

He is not technically a Dreamer. I just don't have a better idea for what to call him. Except, perhaps, for reasons that will become clear, "The Candle."

* * *

Babacar Cisse was raised in Senegal, the former French colony in West Africa. It is a poor, predominantly agricultural country, and his parents were from Kaolack, an inland region that was a common stopping point for traders on their way to Dakar, the capital city on the Atlantic Ocean. Sometime before Babacar was born, they followed those traders and moved to the outskirts of Dakar. Babacar's father ran a small store there, selling goods brought into town from the countryside, and raised a growing family, including his wives and 16 children. Polygamy is legal in Senegal, and a man can marry as many wives as he wishes, but like most men in Senegal, Babacar's father followed the Islamic rule that limits the number of wives to four. Babacar was born to the youngest wife in 1974, the third child and the oldest son among six children in that subset of the family.

"So it was a full house," Babacar recalls. "For a period, there were nine of us sharing one room. We had running water in the neighborhood, but not at home. We didn't have electricity, so you would have to use a candle when you were doing your schoolwork."

That schoolwork was important, because as Babacar puts it, "We were a family of knowledge." Babacar was given the name of his father's father, a well-known religious scholar who taught the Quran to Babacar's father and many others back in their village. "All of his children, including my dad, memorized the Quran," Babacar says. "My dad married fairly late, because he spent his early years just learning. That is what my grandfather wanted— you learn, and then you go out and work and have your family."

Despite the value that Babacar's parents placed on learning, they did not trust the official French-based educational system, nor was there enough money to send their children to regular schools. "It is hard to imagine the suffering and the difficulties they were going through just to pay rent and take us to the hospital if one of us had a scrape," he says. "So my education in primary school was very informal until we moved into a new neighborhood in the suburbs of Dakar. That was when I started in a real school system."

It was May 1985, and Babacar had just turned 11. The new school was Arabic and French, not part of the government-sponsored education system, but a *real* school, with chairs and desks and classrooms. (His previous school had just been a room where all the students sat on the floor together.) The school year was just coming to an end for the other students, and the administrators had to figure out what class to put Babacar in for the rest of the term and the next year.

They took him to the first-grade classroom. There was something written on the blackboard in Arabic, and they asked him to read it. He could. Then they took him to the second-grade classroom, and he could read that blackboard, too. They went to the third-grade classroom, and then the fourth. He read what he could there, and they said, "Maybe this will be the right place for you. Stay here, and next year, you will repeat this grade."

To send Babacar to this school cost his parents about $3 per month—a fee that had risen to about $10 per month by the time he finished high school. As small as this amount of money might seem, it was an excruciating stretch for his parents. His certificate for passing sixth grade was held up because his parents were behind in his tuition.

"My parents didn't have a bank account until I was already out of high school," he says. "That wasn't part of our culture. There wasn't enough money to save. You worked, you earned some money, and then you spent it. And then tomorrow brings what tomorrow brings.

"My mother had six children, and my mom had to make a decision," he says. "It wasn't possible to educate them all. I had older sisters, but they were married. I was older than my younger brother and two younger sisters so I was the one who would get sent to school.

"That meant that I was expected to do really well," he continues. "I had to succeed. My education came at the expense of my younger brother and younger sisters, who actually could not finish school.

"My youngest sister is a thousand times smarter than I am—she was never second in her classes at school. I'm nothing compared to her," Babacar says. "There is a very famous girl's school that people go to after sixth grade. You get in by passing a national exam, and she passed it. But she couldn't go. She had to leave school and she got married when she was 16. The message in the family was that I was the one. They didn't want anything from me but to succeed in school."

He doesn't think he was the chosen one because he was a boy. "It was more age than the fact I was a boy," he says. "If my younger sister had been older than me, I think they would have still invested in me, but I would have gone and found vocational work to help the family. Instead, because I was older and doing well, they focused on educating me."

When Babacar thinks back on that time, he is amazed by how gracefully his parents made painful choices and sacrifices. "I know that they did not sleep well," he says. "They did not spend anything on themselves. They only spent money on us. They felt like they had to do everything they could to take care of the family."

Despite their limited resources, Babacar's parents constantly stressed that doing good for others was a fundamental value of their religion, their culture, their family. "One thing that was very, very clear, throughout my childhood, was the importance of altruism," he says. "My mom used to tell us, 'At some point in your life, you choose to live as a candle.' That meant you light up, and then people can see, even though in the process you might actually disintegrate.

"That's why when you come in here as a neurosurgeon at six in the morning, and sometimes leave the hospital at 3 a.m. because there was an emergency, you don't let it bother you. You are thinking of that patient, and you are thinking about the privilege of taking care of another human being, just like your parents did in very difficult situations."

*   *   *

From the start, Babacar loved school—and his teachers loved him right back. He was smart, worked hard, and had a winning personality. "My mom used to tell me, 'The only thing you're really good at is school, so you had better focus on it,'" he recalls. "The truth is that I was also very good at soccer. And creating trouble at home."

In those last few weeks of fourth grade during that 1985 school year, Babacar showed enough promise that the teacher helped him enroll in some summer classes in areas where he was behind. That allowed him to enroll in fifth grade in the fall—the first but not last time he would have to work hard to catch up in a new educational system.

The classes were taught mostly in Arabic and sometimes in French. In seventh grade, Babacar started to have English classes two hours per week. Looking back, he thinks his education in geography and history was excellent and broader than what US students are exposed to. "We learned a lot of modern history and a lot of ancient history," he says. "My wife is always surprised that I just know facts like Lenin died in 1924 and Stalin died in 1953. There was a lot of religious teaching, but more than that, in social sciences. I feel like we learned about everything."

In the natural sciences, it was another story. "We had no math, physics, or chemistry," he says. "We learned to count, but algebra, trigonometry, calculus, derivatives—I did not study any of that until I came to the United States."

*   *   *

"I graduated from high school in 1993, when I was 19," Babacar says. "And then the problems started."

The most common path for graduates of the Arabic high schools in Senegal was to take an examination. If they passed, they would go to Cairo, Egypt, for university studies. Babacar sat for that examination and did well, so Cairo seemed like the next natural step. But another plan was proposed by a close family friend, an older man in the neighborhood who doted on Babacar. He announced that he had spoken to friends in Morocco and arranged a scholarship for Babacar there. Babacar had two options and thought he should not turn down the family friend's act of generosity. He decided to go to Morocco.

But before Babacar could go, the family friend contracted yellow fever and died. Without that connection, the Moroccan scholarship was given to someone else. The window for the Egyptian option had also closed. Babacar was an unemployed high school graduate with no particular vocational skills, from a poor family in Senegal, and without options or a plan.

"I had to do something useful, and I had to help my mom," he says. He tutored children in Arabic—earning about $20 a month. Meanwhile, he wanted to improve his English, so he started going to the American cultural center and the British Senegalese Institute in Dakar. Throughout the week, the staff at the American center would record the *ABC Evening News with Peter Jennings*, and on Fridays Babacar and others interested in improving their language skills would sit and watch the news of the past week.

Babacar could see that there was a big world out there and started to dream big about where he might go next, even though how he might get there was far from clear. "I thought to myself, 'The sky is the limit,'" he recalls. He started writing away to schools, seeking admission and a scholarship and sending his transcripts with his excellent grades. Many were interested, but the scholarships that were offered were never enough.

"I tried France, and I was admitted to one school, but didn't have the money to go there," he says. "Belgium, same thing.

Norway. England. I tried them all. But I didn't try the United States because I knew it was very expensive, and there was no way for me to pay for four years of education in that country."

* * *

Babacar tried and failed to find a place to go to college for five years. He applied to the local medical school in Senegal. The dean looked at his application and said, "Well, you graduated last year, and we only take people who graduated this year." He was turned down at the local university because it did not recognize the diploma from his private high school.

"Obviously, these things meant a lot of crying, but you can't show people," he says. "Still, when you're sitting by yourself, you have to wonder, 'What am I going to do?'"

Babacar's parents did not want him to give up his dreams of pursuing higher education. "People would tell my parents, 'Look, it's about time you sent this kid to work to help you. He's a full-grown man,'" Babacar recalls. "But no. My parents would say, 'Well, let him try. This is what he wants to do. He wants to focus on education. We'll support him.'" So Babacar did not get a job besides the occasional tutoring, and spent much of his day in the library or at the American cultural center or the British Senegalese Institute.

"I decided that I should start teaching myself science," he recalls. He picked up a copy of the book *The Intelligent Man's Guide to Science* by Isaac Asimov and fell in love with it. Asimov is perhaps most famous as a science fiction writer, but he was also a professor of biochemistry at Boston University, and in the period before he started to earn enough to support himself from fiction writing, he was hired by Basic Books to write a general overview of the sciences. (The audacious title of the book was inspired by George Bernard Shaw's famous 1928 work, *The Intelligent Woman's Guide to Socialism and Capitalism*. Later, Asimov would apologize for the sexism in his title and say that the "man" in the title referred to himself.)

The book is brilliant, really—it provides an easily accessible, sweeping overview of the major advances in several areas of science during the last century. And it inspired Babacar to start reading about physics, chemistry, and other topics. To this day, he likes to read about developments in astrophysics.

He had the curiosity about science of a Renaissance man—but he wasn't living in Europe and it wasn't the Renaissance. The reality was that he was an impoverished young man in West Africa with no obvious path forward. "It was very tough—five years where you feel like you are moving, but there is no clear direction. The only thing you know is that you want to succeed in getting an education," he says. "At the same time, I always had that resilience and that determination that, at some point in time, I was going to get somewhere. For five years, I was basically living on hope."

* * *

Babacar had a cousin who had come to the United States, was living in New York, and had encouraged Babacar to think about coming to America. "Just try it," the cousin said. "There are schools that give out scholarships." That cousin actually paid for Babacar to take the Test of English as a Foreign Language (TOEFL) that is required of foreign students. Babacar did fine on the test thanks to all the time he spent watching Peter Jennings and working on his English over the years.

Babacar started sending out applications to US schools, and the University of Portland, in Oregon, wrote back that he was accepted and offered a partial scholarship. Babacar did not have the money to cover the rest of his expenses, but his cousin said, "Come to the United States. Maybe some people here will help you." And an uncle agreed to go with him to the US embassy and attest that he would help out financially.

It took three trips to the embassy to get the paperwork right. Babacar got his visa on August 8, 1998. It was the day after the terrorist attacks on two US embassies in East Africa—in Dar es Salaam, Tanzania, and Nairobi, Kenya—near-simultaneous truck bombings that were among the first evidence that Osama bin Laden and al-Qaeda were major threats to the US. Security at the US embassy in Senegal was extremely tight when Babacar showed up the next day, and the staff was sending almost everyone away. But one young woman knew Babacar from his previous two visits and said, "OK, come at 4:00, and you can get your visa."

He now had an F1 visa, which requires that he be enrolled as a full-time student. Next, he borrowed money and bought a ticket for August 30, 1998, on Air Afrique, which had direct flights from Senegal to JFK airport. He had never been on an airplane before. He had a window seat and remembers bouncing around, feeling every bit of turbulence while staring out the window at the wing.

"Oh, God," he recalls. "It was quite an experience."

* * *

Babacar had $26 when he landed. He had never seen a credit card or debit card in his life, and didn't even know that they existed. (Islamic law prohibits usury and gambling, which is generally interpreted as forbidding interest on loans.) He did know about taxi cabs, and walked up to a driver and gave him the address of his cousin on Wilson Avenue in the Bronx, near the Boston Post Road.

"There's no Wilson Ave. in the Bronx," the driver said, "you must mean Willis Avenue." (He was referring to a major road in the southern Bronx, far from the Boston Post Road in the northern Bronx.) Babacar said that he had been writing his cousin letters at the Wilson Ave. address, and he had always gotten them. The driver insisted that Babacar's address must be wrong and said he would take him to Willis Ave.

Babacar asked him how much it would cost. The driver said $30.

"I have only $26," Babacar said.

"It's $30," the driver answered.

Babacar paused, and said, "Let's go. My cousin will help me with the remaining $4." And he got into the car, joining other passengers who were going to other destinations in the Bronx.

Babacar was the last passenger to be dropped off, and the driver could not find a Willis Ave. address that made sense, nor could he find any evidence of a Wilson Ave. Enough time had passed that it was now dark. And enough time had passed that the driver and Babacar were starting to become friends.

"Look, here's what we'll do," the driver said. "You can spend the night at my house, and in the morning we'll search for this avenue again."

Babacar agreed. He really had no other options—a hotel was out of the question. The driver, a Gambian, offered Babacar his first American meal—chicken fried rice from a Chinese restaurant.

The next day, the Gambian taxi driver found another taxi driver, this one Hispanic, who knew the various neighborhoods well, and learned that there *was* a Wilson Avenue—it was a short stretch after a bend in a much longer road. They found Babacar's cousin's apartment. Babacar pressed the buzzer, and his cousin appeared. "He paid the driver the 30 bucks," Babacar said. "And it was the beginning of my life in New York City."

* * *

Of course, Babacar did not think he was going to be in New York very long. His plan was to figure out a way to borrow money from relatives or their friends so he could enroll in college in Oregon. "But as soon as I entered the house, I realized that these were people who were working hard, just trying to make a living," he recalls. "There was no way that they could afford that." He called the University of Portland, and they offered him $8,000 in financial aid, but he still had to come up with the rest. When he said that he didn't know how he could do that, they said, "Why don't you stay in New York and try to figure it out. We can defer your admission to the spring."

Babacar talked to another college, Stevens Institute of Technology. Again, he could get partial assistance that was about half of what he needed. As the reality that he could not find a way to borrow enough money set in, he realized that he had two options. He could go home to Senegal, or look for work, which would be in violation of his F1 student visa. He opted for the latter.

He found a job as a busboy at a restaurant in midtown Manhattan, on 49th Street between Madison and Fifth Avenues. There was another man from Senegal working there, and staff who had come from Haiti, Mexico, and Morocco. Like some of them, Babacar was now an undocumented immigrant. When he started working, one of them asked him what he was doing in the United States. He explained that he was trying to go to school. They laughed. "You'll never go to school," one said. "You'll die here. We all came here for school. That is never going to happen."

Babacar would not give in. On his lunch breaks, he would walk to the New York Public Library on 53rd Street between Fifth and Sixth Avenues. He would go to the college handbook sections and search for schools that might give international students a scholarship. That's how he found that Bard College, the private liberal arts school about 120 miles north of New York City, had a Distinguished Scientist Scholarship that would pay full tuition. If Babacar could get it, he would still have to come up with the rest of his expenses, but it was more help than any other school might provide.

He sent in an application, and weeks went by. Then one day when he returned from work, his cousin said, "There was a school that called. They said they wanted to talk to you." His cousin had thought it was a telemarketing ploy of some kind, because Babacar had not told him that was applying to schools. "That's typically how I work," Babacar says. "I try to do things, and don't tell anyone. Then when they pan out, I share the news with my loved ones.

"What's the name of the school?" Babacar asked.

"I don't know," his cousin answered. "I think it starts with a B."

Babacar called Bard the next day and asked if they had been the ones who had called. That is how he learned that he was being considered for the scholarship. "You did really well in high school," the Bard official said. "But you don't quite fit the profile. This program is for people who did well in science in high school, and you didn't have any classes in the sciences. But since you are in New York and not that far away, why don't you come up so we can get to know you?"

Babacar and the official set a date, and Babacar left that day without telling his cousin or his boss at work why he was taking a day off. In his interview with the chair of the biology department, Dr. John Ferguson, they discussed the reality that he had not taken science courses, and thus wasn't really the kind of student for whom the program had been designed.

"Look, I did as much as I could with the opportunities that were presented to me as I was growing up," Babacar said. "If you give me a chance, there is a good possibility that I might do well."

The biology chairman paused and looked at him. Finally he said, "I'll defend you at the committee meeting." And two weeks later, Babacar got a letter saying that he was being admitted to Bard with the scholarship.

It was early spring, but Babacar kept that news a secret until August 1999, shortly before he had to leave. He had started at the restaurant in October 1998, had worked hard, and had received two pay raises. He went to his boss, who had become fond of

Babacar and appreciated how hard he worked. When Babacar told his boss that he was leaving, his boss assumed that Babacar had found a better job, and offered him another raise. Babacar explained that he was going to college, to Bard.

His boss was sad. "It's their gain," he said. "It's our loss, but the college—it's their gain."

Babacar thanked him and then went to the kitchen to tell everyone else that he was leaving. After that, he went home to let his cousin know. And very shortly thereafter, he left for Bard.

* * *

Bard College is in Annandale-on-Hudson, New York, with a beautiful 600-acre campus overlooking the Hudson River and the Catskill Mountains. It was Babacar's first experience in the US countryside. He soon learned that he was the first Senegalese student in its 140-year history. His memory is that the student body was close to 97 percent Caucasian.

But Bard was generous and supportive in every way. Babacar had saved $3,000 from his work as a busboy. The financial aid officer immediately offered loans to cover everything beyond his tuition, which was included in the scholarship. Babacar explained that his immigration status was now a problem, since he had worked illegally. Bard's legal team got to work, and—after a delicate moment or two—Babacar was once again a legal documented alien. (In his second year at Bard, he applied for a green card, and won one through the State Department lottery process.)

"So I started school, and I loved it," he recalls. "I started taking basic math classes—learning calculus, trigonometry, algebra. I took physics and biology. The English classes were very hard for me, and Bard did not have English as a foreign language. I had to learn to write papers for the first time in my life, and I was competing with super-super smart kids. But fortunately, the science came easy to me."

Babacar spent the summer after his first year at the University of Illinois, and the next summer at Harvard School of Public Health. During the third summer, he performed research in a laboratory. By this point, he knew he wanted to pursue research and also become a physician. He applied to MD-PhD programs, and got into one of the most respected in the country—Columbia University.

The idea of becoming a doctor had been in his mind since that five-year period of limbo after high school. Medicine seemed to him the perfect combination of altruism, a core value of his upbringing, and science, for which he had natural talent. "Back in Senegal, when I was alone, I wondered what I could do to help people, and at the same time bring myself happiness. The answer was medicine," he says. "But it just did not seem an option. I was turned down by the medical school in Senegal because of my story. Still, I never gave up on this idea. I knew it could not happen for me in Senegal, but once I reached here, I had to try."

He was six or seven years older than the other students in college, but he did not let that bother him. "There is an Arab poet who says that the heartbeats of a human being are telling him that life is minutes and seconds. So make sure you leave a legacy when you die, because legacy is a second life," he says. "I felt that it didn't matter how long I live or how old I was. What mattered was what I did with my life.

"Besides," he adds, laughing, "Africans tend to look younger than we actually are."

* * *

Even though getting a PhD as well as an MD would delay Babacar's graduation by several years, he was determined to get both degrees because he so enjoyed research. His initial goal was to become an infectious disease specialist and study malaria because of the obvious public health implications. He started a program of immunology research that has been extraordinarily successful, but the science has taken him other directions. Today, he runs a large grant-supported basic science laboratory that studies the interactions between the immune system and brain tumors. The goal of the research is to understand how brain tumors develop and grow, and to work toward identifying targets for treatments that might slow or reverse tumors' progress.

The scientific questions that Babacar found most fascinating steered him toward studying the brain. He decided to go into neurosurgery even though training in that field lasts an average of seven years. Yes, he was off to a late start. He had graduated from high school at 19. He had lost five years trying to get to the United States, and another as an undocumented immigrant working as a busboy. He had spent extra years getting a PhD as well as an MD. But he liked the idea of his clinical work and his research being in the same area.

He enjoyed the residency, but it was hard. "It was like West Point, even worse," he says. "But I learned so much." He trained in a prestigious program at the Weill Cornell Campus of New York Presbyterian Hospital and rotated through Memorial Sloan Kettering Cancer Center. By 2017 Babacar had completed the journey from an informal one-room elementary school to working as a busboy, to training in one of the top neurosurgery programs in the world and serving as its chief resident, to finally joining the staff.

* * *

While still in school, Babacar had married a young woman from Senegal and had three children. But while he was still in training, she decided to take the children back to raise them in their homeland. Today he lives with his second wife and their children in an apartment across the street from the hospital, where he splits his time between running his research program and his clinical care.

He performs a wide range of brain and spine procedures, and has special expertise in primary and metastatic tumors in both regions. The cases are technically challenging, and the diseases often daunting. His hours are long, but by all accounts, Babacar never complains and is unfailingly kind to his patients, and his work is technically excellent.

On the morning that we spoke in his office, he was in scrubs, getting ready to perform an operation on a patient with a large cerebellar mass. He had been asked to perform the procedure by his mentor, Phillip Stieg, the neurosurgeon in chief at Weill Cornell Medical School, with whom he has a very close relationship.

Babacar is aware that part of his success is based upon his intellect, hard work, and resilience, but he knows his journey could not have been successful without unexpected acts from so many and the support of mentor figures like Dr. Stieg. He remembers them all:

- The teacher who helped him go directly from fourth grade to fifth.

- The woman at the embassy who gave him his visa just hours after terrorist attacks elsewhere in Africa.

- His cousin who advised him to apply to US colleges and helped him when he arrived.

- The taxi driver who took him home on his first night in America.

- The many administrators at Bard who bent rules because they recognized his extraordinary potential.

When we talk about the issue of burnout in healthcare, he immediately brings up his parents, and comes back to their constant reinforcement of the importance of being altruistic, no matter how difficult one's own life might be.

"I don't think I have ever thought to myself that I feel burned out," he says. "And I very seldom even feel like I am getting stressed. The reason is that I am here because of choices that I made. No one took my hand and told me that I had to do the things I am doing.

"In medicine, we are so fortunate. We have a world full of opportunities. You can choose anything you want. I picked this, and I said this is what I want to do. I knew it wouldn't be easy. You go through a residency of seven years, where you have people above you, below you, and alongside you that you have to manage. You have patients' families who have expectations, and you have difficult situations when patients are not going to do well. But at the end of the day, we have picked a field in which what really matters is what happens to the patient.

"If I spend 17 hours operating on a patient, doing a big cranial procedure, it often feels like it was just five minutes," he says. "You don't think about the time. You just think about what is happening to them. If I am operating on a young man, I feel like I am operating on my brother. If I am operating on an older woman, I feel like I am operating on my mother. If I'm operating on a child, I'm operating on my son or my daughter.

"As long as I am doing the right thing for my patients, it's like being that candle that I heard about from my parents," he says. "You have to choose to be like a candle, and light up, and help people even if it means you disintegrate. This is the way I have chosen to try to be like a candle. And I'm happy with my choice."

Being and Becoming a Good Doctor

CAN THE STORIES of these seven physicians be more than a collection of stories? Can they collectively provide insight into (1) what it means to be a good doctor in our times, and (2) how to become one?

With those questions in mind, I used a technique for organizing ideas and data developed by Japanese anthropologist Jiro Kawakita that is variably known as the KJ Method or Affinity Diagram. This approach can be helpful for bringing structure to discussions and analyses of topics that are complex and highly vulnerable to biases—like this one. This seems like a fitting place to note that the conclusions in this chapter are offered with appropriate humility. They are based upon seven physicians' stories, interpreted by one author. I have no objection to others collecting and analyzing their own stories and data, and enriching our understanding of what it means to be a good doctor today. In fact, I hope some readers do and would love to see what emerges.

In the KJ Method, you start with data and build up from there. Data in this case are observations of key features of each of the seven doctors' stories. I went through every page of their chapters, and wrote down facts and features of their stories that struck me as relevant to the questions posed previously, for example, "Merit Cudkowicz goes out with team after every clinic session," or "Mike Englesbe was stunned by three consecutive liver donors dying because of prescription opioids."

There were, of course, a lot of observations. But then I started organizing them into natural groupings. For example, Merit is not the only one with close relationships with her team. Mike said his public health work was "propelled by my coworkers." Emily talks about the pride in the cross-training that enables her team to be flexible enough to provide same-day biopsies. These and other observations emerge in Table 9.1 under "Collaborative team-builders."

And then I grouped the groupings, looking for patterns in the "data" that would provide insight. This method is, essentially, thinking—but it's thinking in which the reader can see where the thoughts come from. For example, when I write that these good physicians tend to be collaborative team-builders, you can read specific examples that led to the conclusion and, I hope, bring that conclusion to life.

The three "uber-groupings" that emerged from this exercise examine these questions: (1) What are common work-related characteristics of these seven good doctors? (2) What are common features of their personal makeup? (3) How did they turn out the way they turned out?

Common Work-Related Characteristics

Six common characteristics emerged from the way these seven physicians do their work (Table 9.1). An obvious theme in every portrait is deep empathy for their patients. Like most people in medicine, these seven physicians are highly social creatures; they enjoy their interactions with patients and their colleagues. But these physicians have developed virtuous cycles, in which their empathy for their patients has led to extraordinary things, and those extraordinary things have led to even deeper relationships with their patients.

In some instances, the sources of empathy are painful events from the past that are far from generalizable—for example, Joe Sakran having been shot in the throat as a 17-year-old or Lara Johnson being the child of parents with drug, alcohol, and other problems. In others, empathy flows from the opportunity that every physician has to witness and relate to the suffering of their patients. For example, Babacar Cisse says 17 hours in the operating room can seem like five minutes when he is performing neurosurgery on someone who reminds him of his mother or his children. Mike Englesbe began working on the opioid crisis because of empathy with three patients who were no longer alive—deceased donors for liver transplantation. As he said, "How can you not be moved when there's a naked donor on the table, and you're hearing the story of this young person's journey to death?"

These physicians have the emotional openness to fall in love with their patients and the emotional intelligence to recognize it. And they have acted upon their impulses to do good for their patients in ways that sometimes take them *way* beyond what anyone would consider conventional healthcare. Each step might have seemed logical at the time. For example, Merit felt bad she couldn't see a family of patients with an inherited form of ALS who had become too sick to drive to Boston, so she drove to Connecticut to visit them at home.

For these physicians, step A logically led to B, and B led to C, and C led to D, . . . and suddenly they were doing something completely unexpected. A liver transplant surgeon finds himself leading a public health effort, and a plastic surgeon finds herself running a summer camp for children. All of these physicians went with their instincts, and those instincts took them someplace remarkable.

The resilience these seven people have shown along the way is impressive. No one should think of resilience as a personal characteristic that is the opposite of burnout. Resilience is something that influences how stresses and rewards are experienced, thereby making burnout less likely (see Chapter 1). Greater resilience enables one to respond to stresses, and makes it less likely that one might be crushed by them.

None of these seven has had a smooth and glorious path to success. In fact, how they dealt with setbacks might be the most durable message from their collective stories. Joe's gunshot wound, Babacar's six-year period when there seemed no path to a college education, Lara's whole youth—these challenges might seem too great for readers to imagine enduring. But all of these physicians responded to setbacks, adapted, and persevered. Merit flunked her first test in medical school and has run clinical trials on so many agents that seemed promising for ALS, but ultimately had no benefit. She saves notes from patients—many of whom have passed away from their disease—encouraging her to keep working at finding treatments for ALS.

Mike was very good but not quite great in sports growing up, and that helped prepare him for work in which resilience is such an asset. He is humble enough to know when he has been humbled. When a surgical procedure has a bad outcome, he knows he has something to learn from it. But he is resilient enough to go back into the operating room and perform the next complex surgery.

Laura Monson was told that students from her medical school were never accepted for residency at University of Michigan, and described her reaction as a silent sarcastic one-word thought—"Great." Then she worked her tail off and got in. Later, when she got a telephone call with the news that her dream job had disappeared just a few weeks before it was to start, she put it out of her mind and went back into the operating room to finish the procedure.

Another common characteristic they share is being collaborative and building true teams. I talked with enough of their associates to know that they are *all* really liked and respected by their various colleagues, who are proud to work with them. Merit is aware that her patients with ALS talk to her about their hopes, focusing on the next research trial of a promising agent. But when they meet with the nurse in the next room, they pour out their fears and their anguish. Merit knows that the nurses have the harder role to sustain—that burnout is a bigger threat for them—which is one of the reasons her team goes to an eatery across the street from Massachusetts General Hospital after every patient session to unwind together.

These first four characteristics—empathy, passion, resilience, and a collaborative nature—are integrated with a strong sense of purpose in these physicians. They all see a connection between their work with patients and something bigger. Laura wants to do more than fix the facial anomalies of children; she wants them to have good and rich lives. Merit wants to cure ALS. Mike doesn't want to harvest another liver from someone who died because of prescription opioids ever again. Joe doesn't want people to die from violence of any form. Lara serves the underdog. Emily wants everyone—not just doctors and doctors' families—to receive care that minimizes unnecessary anguish. Babacar feels it is his duty to "choose to live like a candle" and provide light even if it means he disintegrates.

The final characteristic present in many of their stories is the ability to get outraged on behalf of their patients. Table 9.1 shows a sampling of the observations that led to the identification of this characteristic. This set of observations may be a subset of the second category, passion, but "getting mad" seems to imply something beyond deeply caring. The common theme is a fire for reducing the suffering of their patients, and they have used that fire in constructive ways.

Table 9.1.   Common Characteristics

1. Deep empathy
   - Joe Sakran cares for survivors of gun violence, as was he.
   - Mike Englesbe is moved by the stories of young donors' journey to death.
   - Emily Sedgwick knows that when women are told they need to come back into the room for more breast images, "their hearts stop."
   - Lara Johnson is honored to care for people who have the same types of struggles her family faced.
   - Babacar Cisse imagines his patients are members of his immediate family.
   - Laura Monson: can sense how important having friends with similar experiences is to teens with cleft palate.
   - Merit Cudkowicz is able to imagine what patients needed to hear as indicated by her email message, "We are here to help your friend."

2. Passion to go way beyond one's job description
   - Merit drove to Connecticut to see patients who couldn't come to Boston.
   - Emily redesigned breast imaging protocols to reduce patients' fear.
   - Laura started a camp for children with cleft palate.
   - Mike, a transplant surgeon, works on opioid-prescribing patterns.
   - Joe is an advocate for gun violence reduction.

3. Resilience
   - Merit has led so many disappointing drug trials for ALS, but draws resilience from patients—"If they can keep it up, so can we."
   - Mike on being a surgeon: "Surgery is so humbling. . . . You have to be very self-critical, but not let it crack you."
   - Babacar kept looking for a path to education even as an undocumented immigrant working as a busboy.
   - Laura learned her post-fellowship job evaporated as she scrubbed for surgery; she went back into the operating room and finished the procedure.

- Lara graduated valedictorian despite caring for a father with AIDS and dealing with a mother who had major substance-abuse problems.
- Joe decided to use being shot as defining moment to help others.
- Emily didn't give up when the only other MD in her group quit and left.

4. Collaborative team-builders
   - Merit goes out with her team after every patient session.
   - Mike says his work on opioids is "propelled by my collaborators."
   - Laura's camp is staffed by her clinical and nonclinical colleagues, who donate their time.
   - Lara says she doesn't get burned out because she "loves her coworkers."
   - Emily built a team with cross-training and adaptability to give same-day biopsies, when volume fluctuates wildly.

5. Sense of purpose
   - Mike is propelled by the realization that opioid dependence is the most common complication of elective surgery.
   - Merit feels that neuroscience is on the verge of being able to really help patients with ALS and other neurodegenerative conditions.
   - Emily brought breast-imaging redesign to facilities providing care for low-income and uninsured women.
   - Laura wants to make a difference in the long-term outcomes that her patients really care about.
   - Joe sees prevention of gun violence as an extension of his clinical work to help patients who, like himself, have been injured by firearms.
   - Babacar sees it as his duty to "choose to live like a candle," and provide light even if it means he disintegrates.
   - Lara is motivated to give people struggling with addiction and homelessness the same respect and quality of care other patients receive.

6. Ability to get outraged on behalf of patients
   - Merit: "I get mad when I hear about doctors telling patients with ALS that it is hopeless."
   - Emily: "When patients aren't treated well, it really makes me mad."
   - Joe got "incensed" when reading NRA tweet and fired off responses that captured colleagues' emotions.
   - Lara: "It's simplistic to say I always want to root for the underdog, but that's kind of what it feels like."

Personal Makeup

The next uber-grouping of observations relates to their personal makeup (Table 9.2). There is obvious overlap and resonance with the work-related characteristics in Table 9.1, but this is where I put observations that were likely to transcend the work setting. They fell into categories consistent with the four psychological assets that Angela Duckworth has described in her research on grit— interest, purpose, practice, and hope.

Her research has shown that gritty people have both passion and perseverance. They have goals that they *really* care about, and they keep pushing to improve as they pursue those goals for years and decades. They were all willing to make sacrifices along the way. In fact, it's worth noting that *patior*, the Latin root of the word *passion*, implies willingness to sacrifice (e.g., the passion of Christ). It's also worth noting that the word *patient* is derived from the same root and means "one who suffers."

The first psychological asset that helps generate passion is interest. You have to find what you are doing interesting. You have to be curious. You can't yawn and think, "this is one more child with a cleft palate," or "one more woman needing a mammogram," so a box on a list can be checked off. A gritty physician finds their patients interesting and wonders what is really going on in their patients' lives. What are they worried about? How can they be helped?

All seven of these doctors are interested in lots of things— they are naturally curious. Babacar taught himself science during the five years when he couldn't get a formal education, and still reads about astrophysics on his own. Laura's mother was a librarian, and her daughter might have been her most active customer. Merit immersed herself in solving the Rubik's cube with an intensity similar to that she applies to her efforts to find treatments for diseases. Mike wanted numbers to inform his thinking about opioid prescribing, so he worked with a student to find out how many pills were being prescribed by his colleagues—and how many were actually being taken.

The second psychological asset in Angela's framework is purpose—the intention to contribute to the well-being of others. These doctors are idealistic. They are altruistic. They talk about the very clear and compelling messages they received from their parents—for example, Laura's parents urging "to give back," and Emily Sedgwick's parents teaching "to be respectful to all." Babacar and Joe both talked about their grandfathers when I asked them how they turned out the way they are. They felt their grandfathers had made altruism an enduring core value for generations of their families.

This altruism was a common theme even though most of these doctors did not come from privileged backgrounds. Babacar was an immigrant who arrived from Senegal with $26 in his pocket. Joe's father arrived from the Middle East with even less. Mike and Merit, the two with the smoothest paths to medicine, both expressed their sense of obligation to do something meaningful with their education.

These physicians find an outlet for their altruism in their work. If you apply the four questions in Press Ganey's tool for measuring "activation," these physicians would probably have scored quite high at any point in their careers:

1. I care for all patients equally even when it is difficult.

2. I see every patient as an individual with specific needs.

3. The work I do makes a real difference.

4. My work is meaningful.

* * *

The second key component in Angela's grit framework is perseverance, and the first psychological asset in its development is practice. Now "practice" means more than putting in time; it means "deliberate practice" in which you are really trying to get better. You have to have a *growth mindset*, to use the terminology developed by Stanford psychologist Carol Dweck. You have to believe you can get better, and you should get better. Even if you are at the top of your field, you should try to improve. It means being chronically restless and willing to suffer to make progress.

Mike's swimming career presages how he has approached his professional life. He literally plunged into a grueling sport and rose to a high level on the basis of hard work combined with natural gifts, which were considerable but he knew were never going to get him to the Olympics. He realized that one of his core strengths was that he was unafraid to do the hard, grueling thing. He has been drawn to tasks like completing the many years of training in surgery and performing long arduous operations like liver transplants because he knows no one is going to outwork him.

He was not the only competitive person in the group. Laura described herself as being this way as a child—she said she wasn't necessarily trying to beat the other children in spelling bees, but she would be *really* upset if she had not performed her best. My observations of all the rest indicate that they, too, have been ready to do more than put in the hours to learn their crafts. They have pushed themselves to be as good as they could be.

The other psychological asset that contributes to perseverance is hope. As Angela makes clear in her book *Grit*, hope is not optimism that things will get better. It is the belief that things *could* get better if one works hard, learns, and tries new approaches. She invokes the Japanese saying, "Fall seven, rise eight." You keep getting up because you think it might come out differently this time, because you are going to try something different. Angela makes a clear distinction between "I have a feeling tomorrow will be better" and "I resolve to make tomorrow better."

Table 9.2. Personal Makeup

1. Interest
   - Babacar spent five years after high school teaching himself science, and now runs a large immunology/oncology laboratory.
   - Merit spent weeks working on Rubik's cube and decades on research on neurodegenerative diseases.
   - Mike asked medical students to collect data to find out how opioids were being prescribed and used after surgery.
   - Laura feigned illness as a child so she could stay home and read.

2. Purpose
   - Mike describes his sense of duty: "I feel like I have had every opportunity. If I can't be successful in making the world a better place, who can?"
   - Laura internalized her parents' message on the importance of "being a good person and giving back."
   - Emily lives by her parents' counsel to be respectful of everyone and leave things better than she found them.
   - Babacar has adopted his parents' maxim to "live like a candle, and help others even if it means disintegrating."
   - Joe liked helping people as a firefighter and EMT.
   - Merit wanted to solve the energy crisis.

3. Practice
   - Mike swam competitively, determined to be as good as he could be.
   - Laura describes herself as competitive as a young student, wanting to be "as good as I could be."

4. Hope
   - Merit is more excited than ever after two decades of trials of ALS treatments.
   - Mike is sure opioid-prescribing patterns can be improved even more.
   - Laura was ready to start camp without yet having data on long-term outcomes that she hoped to improve.

These physicians all display that second type of hope. Merit is more excited than ever after two decades of trials with ALS treatments. Mike believes that opioid-prescribing patterns can continue to improve. Joe believes that real progress on problems as vexing as gun violence and Middle East peace can occur if people with opposing views listen to each other. Lara believes she can make life a little less painful for homeless and LGBT patients. And so on.

None of them believe that anything is written in stone.

How They Became the Way They Are

Table 9.3 has observations that may help explain how these seven doctors developed the features of their personal makeup summarized in Table 9.2 and the work-related characteristics in Table 9.1. All seven are tuned into the importance of families—those of their patients' as well as their own. For example, when Merit talks about the size of her ALS program, she routinely says, "We take care of 500 families." This isn't lip service. As described in her chapter, her program has added a psychiatrist to help patients with ALS and their spouses talk to their children. And Joe, Babacar, and Lara all made comments about how, when taking care of their patients and talking to patients' families, they routinely had thoughts about their own.

They all spoke with pride and appreciation about their families and the values they had learned from their parents. They talked about the emphasis on education, whether in West Africa or western Michigan. Some of their parents were, as Joe put it, "deeply involved" in their children's educations. Merit's mother would call her daughter at four in the morning to be sure she had woken up in time to go to surgery rounds. Mike thinks teaching medical students and residents comes naturally to him because his mother was a teacher.

They told vignettes illustrating how their parents taught them to be independent—like Lara's father encouraging her drive at age 12 and Mike's father dropping him off at school with the message that if adjusting was difficult, he shouldn't think coming home was an option. And as already noted, many of them explicitly cite altruism as a core value emphasized by their parents.

They had other role models and mentors, including physicians who made a real difference during serious illnesses of members of their families, and teachers who took a strong interest in them. Laura is still grateful to her third-grade teacher, who started a club for gifted children and taught them to build and launch rockets in the era of the space shuttles. Emily still appreciates the impact of her sixth-grade teacher, who treated her like an adult; he had gone to Berkeley, so she wanted to, too. And of course, Lara's high school teacher completely changed her life by paying her college tuition.

Perhaps these physicians had the good fortune to run into great mentors when they were young. But it is also possible that some qualities made them wonderful mentees. Probably both are true.

As noted in Table 9.3, they have moved around and been exposed to multiple cultures and influences; none of the physicians in this series live in the same town as their parents or grandparents. Babacar is an immigrant, and Joe and Merit are the children of immigrants. Mike is married to a Chinese American, and Emily Sedgwick is married to a Mexican American. It seems reasonable to wonder if variability in the cultural influences in their lives contributes to openness in their thinking about the nature of their work.

On the other hand, this degree of cultural heterogeneity may be within statistical norms for US medicine in our times. It is a good field for immigrants and their children, and residency (where both Mike and Emily met their spouses) is an ideal setting for hard workers to realize they have much in common, even if their ethnic backgrounds do not match.

As a group, these seven doctors seemed unusually self-aware—one of the qualities psychologist Daniel Goleman identifies as key ingredients of emotional intelligence. They know their own strengths, weaknesses, values, and impact on others. In fact, they displayed strength on all five of the attributes Goleman says constitute emotional intelligence; the other four are self-regulation (controlling or redirecting disruptive impulses and moods), motivation (relishing achievement), empathy (understanding other people's emotional makeup), and social skill (building rapport with others to move them in desired directions).

Finally, they all displayed a growth mindset. They believed that things could and should get better, and they were willing to work hard and sacrifice to make that happen.

Table 9.3.　How They Became the Way They Are

---

1. They are attuned to families.
   - Merit: "We take care of 500 families."
   - Joe thinks about impact of trauma/violence on families of patients.
   - Babacar sees his family members in his patients.
   - Lara said, "I have the privilege of taking care of patients with the same challenges as my parents."

---

2. They are aware and proud of values important in their own families.
   - Babacar: "We are a family of knowledge."
   - Mike feels like teaching students comes naturally to him because his mother is a teacher.
   - Lara's father emphasized independence and made her drive when she was 12 years old.
   - Joe feels that his grandfather in Nazareth set an example for him as community-minded leader, even though they never met.
   - Emily sent an email with a final thought: "My mom taught me to leave a place better than I found it."
   - Merit's mother would call her to make sure she woke up in time for rounds.
   - Laura's mother was a librarian, and Laura became an avid reader.

3. They were open to the influence of mentors and role models.
   - Laura was impressed by the family practitioner who cared for her mother when she had breast cancer.
   - Laura's third-grade teacher was first to tell her she should go to college.
   - Emily's sixth-grade teacher had gone to Berkeley and made her want to, too.
   - Lara never forgot the Parkland neurosurgery fellow who treated her mother with respect.
   - Lara's high school teacher got her to apply to college and paid her tuition.
   - Mike met a transplant surgeon when he was in seventh grade and decided he wanted to be a transplant surgeon.
   - Babacar developed multiple close relationships, including with the current neurosurgeon-in-chief.

4. They have been exposed to multiple cultures.
   - Babacar is an immigrant who was undocumented for a while.
   - Joe is the son of Lebanese immigrants from Israel.
   - Merit is the daughter of Italian immigrants.
   - Mike is married to a Chinese American.
   - Emily is married to a Mexican American.

5. They are self-aware.
   - Emily was embarrassed by having two standards of care.
   - Mike knew he wasn't going to be an Olympian.
   - Babacar knows he makes friends easily.
   - Joe's hands were shaking when he worked in front of surgeons who, years before, had saved his life.

6. They have a growth mindset.
   - Laura is the first in her family to go to college, and graduated summa.
   - Lara is first in her family to go to college, and graduated summa.
   - Joe took major pay reduction so he could attend Harvard's Kennedy School of Government.
   - Emily refused to accept status quo of breast imaging.
   - Mike wants to learn how to eliminate opioid prescribing for many surgical patients.

* * *

What have we learned from these good doctors? The obvious starting point is we are fortunate to have them among us. Their stories are extraordinary, but in fact, their strengths are not. They don't think of themselves as special. They all describe themselves as "lucky."

They are all smart, but intelligence is not what sets them apart. They all work hard, but so do many others in medicine. In fact, I was impressed by the extent to which these doctors find the time for lives outside their work. Merit had to delay an interview because she was playing in a soccer game. Joe's interview was squeezed in during a visit to his parents. Emily had just taken her kids swimming. In every one of my interviews, it felt like family was lurking just out of sight or hearing range. And often, children interrupted, doors slammed, and the physicians were summoned by loved ones to come eat.

The characteristics that emerged from the analysis of their stories, summarized in Tables 9.1 to 9.3, are actually quite common among people working in healthcare. However, these physicians seem to have them in unusual abundance. Pretty much every physician or nurse I know delivers care with empathy, goes beyond their job description, and is a good team member at least some of the time—but perhaps not with the reliability of these seven doctors or to the same extent.

The implication is that healthcare offers clinicians opportunities to do extraordinary things—and these physicians have recognized those opportunities and seized them. They have the same generous instincts as the rest of us; they have just been more diligent in following them.

They were all fortunate to be in circumstances in which it was possible for them to be their best selves. Although they might have had difficult circumstances in youth or encountered obstacles along the way, they all work in organizations that have supported their desires to follow their best instincts.

Massachusetts General Hospital has essentially given Merit the message, "Figure out what is the best possible care for your ALS patients, and we will figure out how to make it work." (It's probably not quite that simple, but it seems pretty close.) Michigan Medicine CEO Marschall Runge is proud that his highly trained transplant surgeon is working on a public health problem. Texas Children's encourages employees to donate time to Laura's camp. Parkland Hospital wants to give good care to homeless and LGBT patients, and its leaders are delighted to support Lara in that work.

One takeaway from this book for leaders of healthcare: If you want good physicians like these, just give them the chance to emerge. They are there. I know they will step forward and make you and your organizations proud.

To mitigate physician burnout, organizational leaders should work on reducing the burdens not directly connected to patient care—the "external stresses" described in Chapter 1. But leaders should also help physicians find meaning in their work. Providing physicians with the opportunity to be at their best is more than being nice; it is strategic. This is a way in which you articulate your values and make your personnel proud to be part of the organization. And that pride has direct business performance rewards. You have less turnover, better safety, better patient experience, and better technical quality. (Trust me, the data are there.)

For my colleagues who are physicians, and the students who seek to become one, my expectation is that these seven good doctors seem familiar. You probably all know physicians like them. In fact, there is a chance that others think of you in the same way.

What I like about medicine and what makes it so challenging is that you are starting from scratch with every patient. It doesn't matter if you have done a fantastic job technically with every patient in the past 10 years; if you relax and provide care that is unsafe with the next patient, the result can be catastrophic. It doesn't matter if your survey ratings yield a magnificent set of numbers; if you are in a foul mood and behave like a jerk with your next patient, you are a jerk.

The past is the past. The future is what matters. It's all about the next patient you see. And that next patient offers the chance to be a good doctor.

How great is that?

Notes

1. Thomas H. Lee and Deirdre Mylod, "Deconstructing Burnout to Define a Positive Path Forward," *JAMA Internal Medicine* 179, March 2019: 429–430. DOI:10.1001/jamainternmed.2018.8247.
2. Melinda Ashton, "Getting Rid of Stupid Stuff," *New England Journal of Medicine* 379, November 8, 2018: 1789–1791. DOI:10.1056/NEJMp1809698.
3. Colin P. West, Liselotte N. Dyrbye, Jeff T. Rabatin, Tim G. Call, John H. Davidson, Adamarie Multari, Susan A. Romanski, Joan M. Henriksen Hellyer, Jeff A. Sloan, and Tait D. Shanafelt, "Intervention to Promote Physician Well-being, Job Satisfaction, and Professionalism," *JAMA Internal Medicine* 174, April 2014: 527–533. DOI:10.1001/jamainternmed.2013.14387.
4. *Empathy: The Human Connection to Patient Care*, https://www.youtube.com/watch?v=cDDWvj_q-o8).
5. Grady Health System, https://www.glassdoor.com/Reviews/Employee-Review-Grady-Health-System-RVW21101548.htm, accessed February 17, 2019.
6. Deirdre E. Mylod and Thomas H. Lee, "Helping Health Care Workers Avoid Burnout," *Harvard Business Review*, published online October 12, 2018, https://hbr.org/2018/10/helping-health-care-workers-avoid-burnout.
7. Thomas H. Lee and Angela L. Duckworth, "Organizational Grit," *Harvard Business Review* 96, September–October 2018: 98–105.
8. Megan L. Ranney, Marian E. Betz, and Cedric Dark, "#ThisisOurLane—Firearm Safety as Healthcare's Highway," *New England Journal of Medicine* 380, January 31, 2019: 405-407. DOI: 10.1056/NEJMp1815462

Index

ABC Evening News with Peter Jennings, 137
Activation:
  and altruism, 157
  for good doctors, 11–14
Adams, Raymond, 41
Addiction:
  cycles of, 110–111
  and prescription drugs, 20
Adverse childhood experiences, 109–111, 117–118
Affinity Diagram, 149
Aguilar, David, 59–60
Ahmed, Robert, 76–77, 81
AIDS epidemic, in San Francisco, 58
Alcoholism, 115
ALS (*see* Amyotrophic lateral sclerosis)
Altruism:
  as family value, 135
  of profiled doctors, 157

American College of Surgeons, 85
Amherst Central High School (Buffalo, New York), 36
Amyotrophic lateral sclerosis (ALS), xi, 35, 42–51
Annals of Internal Medicine, 70
Annandale-on-Hudson, New York, 144
Antisense oligonucleotide, 50
Arnold P. Gold Foundation Humanism in Medicine Award, 25
Asimov, Isaac, 138–139
"Atlanta Can't Live Without Grady" campaign, 10–11

Baltimore VA Medical Center, 125
Bard College, 132, 142–144
Baylor College of Medicine (BCM), 54–56, 60, 67

Bella Vista High School (Sacramento, California), 57
Ben-Gurion University, 79–80
Biomedical engineering, 37
Biopsy, breast, 55–56, 61
Blue Cross Blue Shield, 29
Borderline Bar and Grill shooting (Thousand Oaks, California), 70
Breast imaging, xii, 53–54, 64
Breast imaging fellowship program, 64
Breast MRI program, 64
Brigham and Women's Hospital, 41, 59
Brown, Robert, 42, 44
Brummett, Chad, 27
Buffalo, New York, 36
Burnout:
and activation, 13–14
among medical professionals working with underserved populations, 113
Babacar Cisse on, 147–148
Merit Cudkowicz on, 48
epidemic of, among doctors, xiii, xv, 3–5
Lara Johnson on, 127–128
of nurses, 153
and resilience, 4–11

Joseph Sakran on, 86–87
Burton, Texas, 104

Cairo, Egypt, 137
Camp Keep Smiling, 91, 104–105
Chaotic home environment, 110–111, 117, 119
Charleston, South Carolina, 83
Cisse, Babacar, 131–148, 151, 156, 157
Cleveland Clinic, 8, 9–10
Columbia University, 132, 145
Communications, with patients, 64
Complexity, of modern medicine, 1–2
Cosgrove, Toby, 9–10
Cotton Bowling Palace, 115–116
Cross-training, 63–64
Cudkowicz, Merit, xi–xii, 33–51, 151–153, 156, 157, 159–160, 165
Cultural diversity, exposure to, 161, 163t
Curiosity, 156–157

Dakar, Senegal, 133
Decompression, 11–14
Detroit, Michigan, 96

Development, Relief, and Education for Alien Minors (DREAM) Act, 131

Diagnostic mammograms, 55

Dodge, Elizabeth, 125

Donors, of organs, 19–20

DREAM (Development, Relief, and Education for Alien Minors) Act, 131

Duckworth, Angela, xv, 14, 16, 156, 158

Dweck, Carol, 16, 158

East Dallas, Texas, 109

Education:
    importance of, 133–134, 160
    in Senegal, 136

Education Advisory Committee, 25

Electronic medical records (EMRs), 2–3

Emotional intelligence, 162

Empathy, 150–151, 154*t*

Empathy video (Cleveland Clinic), 9–10

EMRs (electronic medical records), 2–3

Engagement, 13

Englesbe, Mike, 19–31, 151, 152, 156–161

Faherty, Patricia, 111–113, 120–121, 128

Fakhry, Samir, 83

Falls Church, Virginia, 74

Families:
    of doctors, 160–161, 162*t*, 164
    of gun violence victims, 77–78
    of patients, 38, 46, 160, 162*t*

Family practice, 124

Fear, reducing, 67–68

Ferguson, John, 143

FierceHealthcare, 72

Financial barriers, to same-day biopsies, 61

Firefighting, 79

Fisher, C. Miller, 41

Fixed mindset, 16

Fort Worth, Texas, 124

Fundraising, 104

Gallbladder removal (laparoscopic cholecystectomy), 28–29

George Mason University, 79

Georgetown University, 125

Gerber, David, 125

Get Rid of Stupid Stuff (GROSS) program, 8, 14

Global Disaster Preparedness for the Department of Surgery, 83
Goal hierarchy, 15–16
Goleman, Daniel, 162
Good doctors, 1–17, 149–166
  activation and decompression for, 11–14
  burnout and resilience, 4–11
  development of, 160–166
  and grit, 14–17
  in modern medicine, 1–3
  personal makeup of, 156–160
  work-related characteristics of, 150–155
Good Shepherd Hospice, 126
Grady Health System, 10–11
Gratefulness, 128
Grit:
  of Merit Cudkowicz, 39
  and good doctors, 14–17
  passion and perseverance as key ingredients of, xv
  psychological assets in, 156
Grit (Duckworth), 158
Gross, Terry, 72
GROSS (Get Rid of Stupid Stuff) program, 8, 14
Growth mindset, 16, 158, 162, 163t

Gun control advocacy, 69–70, 85
Gun violence, xiii, 69–73, 75–76, 81–82

HAART (highly active antiretroviral therapy), 58
Harris Health System, 65–67
Harvard Medical School, 38–39
Harvard–MIT Program in Health Sciences and Technology (HST), 38
Hawaii Pacific Health, 8
Healey, Sean, xi, 44
Highly active antiretroviral therapy (HAART), 58
Hollier, Larry, 101–104
Homeless Outreach Medical Services (HOMES), 113
Hope, 158–160, 159t
"How a Teacher Changed This Dallas Doctor's Life" (Thompson), 114
HST (Harvard–MIT Program in Health Sciences and Technology), 38
Huntington's disease, 41

Identification, with group, 17

IHPI (Institute for Healthcare Policy and Innovation), 27

Illnesses, of parents, 110–111, 118

Immigrants, 131–132, 161

Information technology, 2–3

Inova Fairfax Hospital, 74, 76, 80–81

Institute for Healthcare Policy and Innovation (IHPI), 27

The Intelligent Man's Guide to Science (Asimov), 138

Interest, 156–157, 159*t*

Interventions, to increase resilience, 8–10

Israel, 33, 73–74, 79–80, 83–84

Israeli-Palestinian violence, 80

Italy, 36

Jerusalem, Israel, 80

John Peter Smith Family Practice Residency, 124

Johns Hopkins Hospital, 69–70, 84, 125

Johns Hopkins University, 83

Johnson, Lara, xii–xiii, 109–129, 151, 152, 153, 157, 160, 161

Kawakita, Jiro, 149

Kennedy School of Government, 83

KJ Method, 149–150

Lake Braddock Secondary School (Burke, Virginia), 75

Langer, Robert, 38, 49

Laparoscopic cholecystectomy (gallbladder removal), 28–29

Leadership skills, 62, 127

Leonard Tow Humanism in Medicine Award, 25

Management skills, 63

Maslach Burnout Index, 11

Massachusetts General Hospital (MGH), 40–44, 165

Massachusetts Institute of Technology (MIT), 36–38

Mayo Clinic, 8

McBride, Timothy, 77

Medical University of South Carolina, 83

Memorial Sloan Kettering Cancer Center, 146

Memphis, Tennessee, 122

Mentors, 161, 163*t*

MGH (*see* Massachusetts General Hospital)
Miami, Florida, 74
Michigan, 19
Michigan Medicine, 28–29, 165
Michigan Opioid Prescribing and Engagement Network, 30
Michigan Surgical Quality Collaborative, 30
Mickey, Bruce, 118
Mindfulness training, 5
MIT (Massachusetts Institute of Technology), 36–38
Monson, Laura, xiv, 89–107, 152–153, 156, 158, 161
Moskowitz, Mike, 39
Mukherjee, Dipankar, 77, 81
Mylod, Deirdre, 5, 12

National Public Radio, 72
National Rifle Association (NRA), 69–71
Network (film), 72
Neuroscience, 39–40
New England Journal of Medicine, 72
New York City, New York, 131, 140–141
New York Presbyterian Hospital, 132, 146

New York Public Library, 132, 142
New York Times, 72
Newman, Haskell, 97–98
NRA (National Rifle Association), 69–71
NurOwn, 34–35

Oak Ridge, Tennessee, 36
Opioid addiction, 20
Opioid epidemic, 27–28
Opioid overdoses, 26
Optimism, 158
Organ transplantation:
  donor honored in, 19–20
  education for, 22–23
"Organizational Grit" (Duckworth and Lee), 15
Organizations:
  clinicians' identification with, 9
  doctors supported by, 165
  grit for, 15
  stresses alleviated by, 11

Parkland Health and Hospital System, 109, 112, 113, 118, 125–126, 165
Passion:
  of Merit Cudkowicz, 50–51
  as key ingredient of grit, xv

leading to unexpected
activities, 151–152
as work-related characteristic, 154*t*
Pat Korell Endowed
Professorship in Breast
Imaging, 65
Patient advocacy, 153, 155*t*
Patient care, 5–6
in breast imaging, 67–68
emotional toll of, 47–48
enjoyment of, 40
and trust of patients, 126
Patient centered care, 33–35,
41, 42, 45–46
Patient engagement, 3
Patient-reported outcome
measures (PROMs), 90,
102–103
Pediatric plastic surgery, 97–98
Perseverance:
as key ingredient of grit, xv
and practice, 157–158
Personal characteristics, 156–
160, 159*t*
Plastic surgery, 97
Practice, 158, 159*t*
Prescription drugs, 20, 27–29
Press Ganey, 11, 157
Primary care medicine, 96–97
PROMs (patient-reported
outcome measures), 90,
102–103

Public policy, 86

Quality of life improvements,
103–104

Rauch, Paula, 38, 46
Raymond, Ohio, 56
Reeths-Puffer High School
(Twin Lake, Michigan),
91
Resilience:
and burnout, 4–11
and grit, 16
of Laura Monson, 99–100
of profiled doctors,
152–153
as requirement for sur-
geons, 23
as work-related characteristic, 154*t*–155*t*
Respect:
learning at young age, 57
for patients, 126–127
Rewards:
commingled with stresses, 6
intervention to increase,
8–9
Robert Wood Johnson
Medical School, 22
Role models, 161, 163*t*
Roy, Michelle, 105
Rubik, Ernō, 37
Rubik's cube, 37

Ruby, Jack, 115–116
Runge, Marschall, 165
Ryan, Pat, xi–xii

St. Joseph's Preparatory
    School (Philadelphia),
    21
Sakran, Joseph, xiii, 69–87,
    151, 157, 159–160
Sakran, Victor, 73, 74
Same-day biopsies, 61
Screening mammograms, 55
Sean M. Healey & AMG
    Center for ALS at Mass
    General, 44–45, 50
Second Intifada, 80
Sedgwick, Emily, xii, 53–68,
    150, 153, 157, 161, 164
Self-awareness, 163t
    of problems in routine care,
        54
    of profiled doctors, 162
    of surgery performance,
        23
Senegal, 133
Sense of purpose:
    for Babacar Cisse, 148
    for Mike Englesbe, 30–31
    as personal characteristic,
        157, 159t
    of profiled doctors, 153
    provided by organizations,
        165

and resilience, 9–10
    for Joseph Sakran, 87
    as work-related characteris-
        tic, 155t
Sharon, Ariel, 80
Smith, Lester, 65–66
Smith Clinic, 66
Social networks, 25–26
Social outcomes, for children
    with cranio-facial
    conditions, 90–91
Socialization:
    among children with
        similar conditions,
        91, 104
    among clinicians, 8–9
SOD1 mutation, 42–43, 48,
    49–50
Sorets, Eugene, 43, 49
Sports, involvement in,
    20–22
Stieg, Phillip, 147
Stevens Institute of
    Technology, 142
Stresses:
    leading to burnout, 5–14
    in medical field, xiii–xiv
    removing preventable, 14
Swimming, 21–22, 158

Teaching, 24–25, 29
Team collaboration:
    by good doctors, 2, 15

in pediatric cranio-facial surgery, 102–103
by profiled doctors, 153
by Emily Sedgwick, 62
as work-related characteristic, 155*t*
Teams, grit for, 15
Tele-medicine, 45–46
Test of English as a Foreign Language (TOEFL), 139
Texas Children's Cleft Lip and Palate Clinic, 91
Texas Children's Hospital, 89, 90, 101–102, 165
#ThisIsOurLane, xiii, 71–72, 85–86
Thompson, Jamie, 114
Thousand Oaks, California, 70
TOEFL (Test of English as a Foreign Language), 139
Tragedy, responses to, 78–79
Transgender clinic, 126
Trauma Center at Penn Presbyterian Medical Center, 81–82
Trinity University, 121
Twin Lake, Michigan, 91
Twitter, xiii, 69–71

UCSF (University of California, San Francisco), 58

Underserved populations, 113
University of Buffalo, 36
University of California, Berkeley, 57–58
University of California, San Francisco (UCSF), 58
University of Illinois, 145
University of Memphis, 122–123
University of Michigan, 20, 30, 97, 98
University of Michigan Health System, 24
University of Pennsylvania, 20, 21
University of Pittsburgh Medical Center (UPMC), 99
University of Portland, 139, 142
University of Texas at Arlington, 123
University of Texas Southwestern Medical School, 112, 123, 125–126
University of Washington, 24
UPMC (University of Pittsburgh Medical Center), 99

Volunteer work, at clinic,
94–95
Voorhees, New Jersey, 20

Waljee, Jennifer, 27, 28
Washington Post, 72
Wayne State University
School of Medicine, 96,
98
Weill Cornell Medical
College, 132, 146

Western Michigan University,
93–94
Woodrow Wilson High
School (East Dallas,
Texas), 109, 111–113,
115–116
Work-related characteristics,
150–155, 154*t*–155*t*
Wu, Audrey, 24

Yale University, 22, 125

About the Author

Thomas H. Lee, MD, is chief medical officer of Press Ganey Associates, Inc. He is a practicing primary care physician and cardiologist at Brigham and Women's Hospital, and a professor of medicine (part-time) at Harvard Medical School and professor of health policy and management at the Harvard School of Public Health.

Before assuming his role at Press Ganey, he was network president for Partners Healthcare System, the integrated delivery system founded by Brigham and Women's Hospital and Massachusetts General Hospital. He is a graduate of Harvard College, Cornell University Medical College, and Harvard School of Public Health.

Dr. Lee is a member of the board of directors of Geisinger Health System, the board of directors of Health Leads, the board of overseers of Weill Cornell Medical College, the Special Medical Advisory

Group (SMAG) of the Veterans Administration, and the Panel of Health Advisors of the Congressional Budget Office.

He also serves on the editorial board of the *New England Journal of Medicine*. He is the author, with James J. Mongan, MD, of *Chaos and Organization in Health Care*, the author of *Eugene Braunwald and the Rise of Modern Medicine* and *An Epidemic of Empathy in Healthcare*, and the coeditor, with Joseph Cabral and Martin Wright, of *The Engaged Caregiver*.

About Press Ganey

THE GOOD DOCTOR

P RESS G ANEY was founded more than 30 years ago, based on a passion to help improve the way in which healthcare is delivered. Today, that principle remains a core element of Press Ganey's mission to help health-care organizations across the continuum reduce suffering and enhance caregiver resilience to improve the safety, quality, and experience of care.

Press Ganey partners with providers to capture the voices of patients, physicians, nurses, and employ-ees to gain insights to address unmet needs. Through the use of integrated data, advanced analytics, and strategic advisory services, Press Ganey helps clients transform their organizations to deliver safer, high-quality, patient- and family-focused care.

Press Ganey is recognized as a pioneer and thought leader in healthcare performance improvement solu-tions. As a strategic business partner to more than 41,000 healthcare organizations, Press Ganey leads the industry in helping clients drive enterprise trans-formation across the patient journey.

For more information, please visit pressganey.com.

Also from Press Ganey

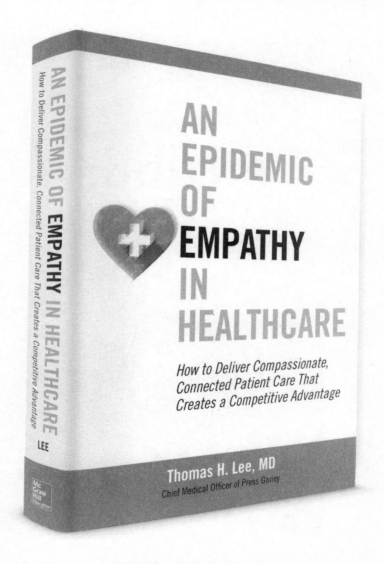

978-1259583018

Also from Press Ganey

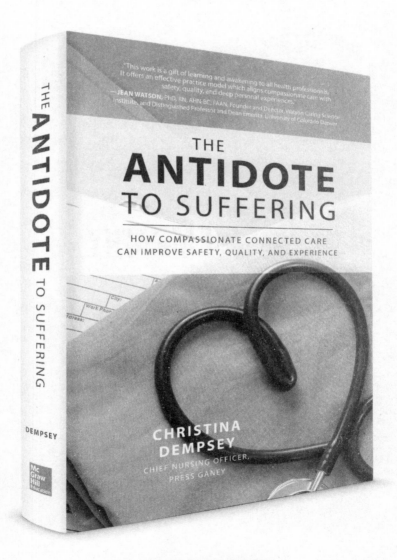

978-1260116557

Because learning changes everything.*

Also from Press Ganey

"A turning point in patient safety, this book will unleash the power and talent of health systems in pursuit of transformative safety and experience."

—A. MARC HARRISON, MD, President and CEO, Intermountain Healthcare

ZERO HARM

HOW TO ACHIEVE PATIENT AND WORKFORCE SAFETY IN HEALTHCARE

Edited by

Craig Clapper, PE
James Merlino, MD
Carole Stockmeier
of Press Ganey

978-1260440928

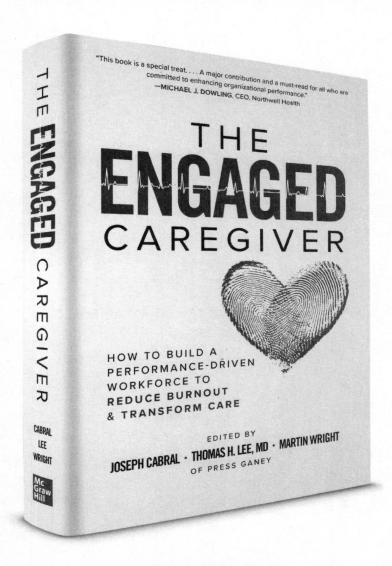